UNION
QUALITY

UNION QUALITY
THE STORY OF COUNCIL 2

Exceptional American workers and those who have inspired them

WASHINGTON STATE
COUNCIL OF COUNTY AND CITY EMPLOYEES
AFSCME   AFL-CIO

The Washington State Council of County and City Employees
AFSCME, AFL-CIO

GRAHAM FYSH

Published by LifeTime Creations, Sequim, Washington
http://www.lifetimecreations.com
Printed in the United States
ISBN: 978-0-9628987-6-1

LIFETIME
CREATIONS

Also available as an e-book. See http://www.unionquality.org

A STORY OF OUTSTANDING ACHIEVEMENT

AT A TIME WHEN labor unions are under attack across the United States and the rate of union membership is close to an all-time low, the Washington State Council of County and City Employees, AFSCME, AFL-CIO (Council 2) stands out. In sharp contrast with the overall trend, its membership is strong and it continues to grow.

It is the epitome of what a successful union should be.

This book tells the story of how the union became so successful. But it does more than outline its history. It also provides an insight into the people who make up Council 2 — its outstanding leaders and members, many of whom have given decades of superior service to their cities and counties and who have gone the extra mile to help fellow members as well as others in their community.

This insight into the life of Council 2 has been compiled from a variety of sources — interviews, personal reminiscences, newsletters and newspapers. Some of the profiles have appeared in Council 2 publications over the years; many have been written especially for this book.

ABOUT COUNCIL 2

The Washington State Council of County and City Employees, (WSCCCE) AFSCME, AFL-CIO represents local government employees who provide services to the citizens of Washington state.

It is a democratic union providing a real voice for its members through active participation and professional representation. The union works to preserve and enhance workers' compensation and benefits. It also promotes job security and improves other employment conditions.

Members in 2015: 17,000
Local unions represented: 170
About 280 contracts negotiated and settled every three years.

Contents

Our union goes back a long way

BY CHRIS DUGOVICH
COUNCIL 2 PRESIDENT/EXECUTIVE DIRECTOR

Ever since it started in 1937, the Washington State Council of County and City Employees, AFSCME, AFL-CIO has been working on behalf of local government employees to retain and enhance their rights as public employees.

When our charter was granted by the American Federation of State County and Municipal Employees, the local unions were directly chartered through the International Union without a state council.

A handful of our local unions existed even before AFSCME's creation and were chartered directly from the AFL-CIO.

After the creation of Council 2, the initial job of the new organization was to affiliate with the state council all the then existing locals. Local 120 Pierce County-City of Tacoma, Local 109 Snohomish County Roads, Local 113 City of Everett, and Local 87 Yakima County, just to name a few, were all part of this process.

In the early 1950s, gains that the union made included allowing local government employees to participate in the Public Employment Retirement System and Social Security. Until then, it was not even an option to participate and only the larger jurisdictions had set up their own retirement systems. Some still exist in Tacoma, Seattle and Spokane.

From 1951 to 1957, Orville Swartz, a City of Spokane employee, served as president of Council 2. In 1957, Gerry Burke, the president of Snohomish County Roads Local 109, served a two-year term. In 1961, the Council

---

BEING A MEMBER of the **American Federation of State County and Municipal Employees** (AFSCME) always has been an outstanding benefit to Council 2.

The organization has provided support in tough situations, given valuable advice, and made available senior officials to assist the union. Council 2 is also grateful for the encouragement and assistance provided by its exceptional presidents, notably Gerald McEntee (1981–2012) and Lee Saunders (2013–present).

2 convention changed its constitution in reaction to its growing membership of 2,000 local government employees and elected its first full-time President/Executive Director, Sam Kinville.

All local government employees

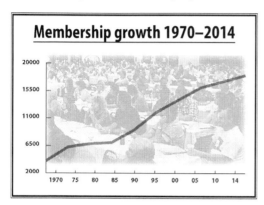

Membership growth 1970–2014

continue to benefit from Sam's foresight. In 1966 he lobbied for, and gained passage of RCW 41.56, the collective bargaining law that has served us well during the past 44 years.

If you think about the difficulties of organizing or gaining wage or benefit increases without any legal obligation whatsoever for the employer even to discuss these issues, you know how significant and important the collective bargaining law has been. The rights embodied in law have served us well both in good times and tough times. *(A report on the law is on page 16.)*

Sam served until he accepted a position in the Washington State Labor Council and the union elected Larry McKibben, a member of the staff, to the position of president/executive director.

Larry served in the position until his retirement in the fall of 1989 and guided the union through negotiations of its first contracts under the collective bargaining law and brought its membership to about 7,800. He also served a term as an AFSCME International vice-president.

In the Fall of 1989 I became President/Executive Director of Council 2.

We now boast about 17,000 members statewide.

The real history of the union involves the countless number of grievances settled and won that have saved jobs and all the contracts settled that, sometimes slowly, but always surely, have made local government employment an excellent profession.

This union is the reason our membership has a retirement plan, health insurance and the ability to bargain collectively.

It is also why, however impossible it's been to save all the jobs, we've been able to save so many during the tough times.

In the pages ahead you'll read of the victories, the tough times and the fun times. You'll find the stories, too, of people who have contributed so much to the union, as leaders and as members, doing their daily work.

Of course, these are only some of the stories. To record them all would take a really thick book!

We thank all our members for their dedication, determination and devotion.

They are indeed quality people.

Winning the fight

Improving members' working conditions year after year

I n this section we highlight significant events in Council 2's history over the years since its formation, showing how it became the strong and effective union it is today.

Included are profiles of leaders, interesting vignettes and humorous sidelights.

The accounts have been compiled from interviews with union members and leaders, minutes recorded since the union's formation, and publications produced by the union over the years.

Council 2 Presidents

C.E. Anderson 1937–1944

C.M. Hiberly 1944–1951

Orville A. Swartz 1951–1957

Gerald A. Burke 1957–1959

Sam Kinville... 1959–1967

Larry McKibben 1967–1989

Chris Dugovich 1989–present

AFSCME Presidents

Arnold Zander 1936–1964

Jerry Wurf 1964–1981

Gerry McEntee.. 1981–2012

Lee Saunders 2013–present

1937

Council 2 is first union to be established under AFSCME

A union to represent county and city employees in Washington State is formed in 1937 under the umbrella of the American Federation of State County and Municipal Employees (AFSCME), which had been established on September 17, 1936 out of the American Federation of Labor (AFL)with Arnold Zander as first International President.

The Washington state union includes a handful of local unions that already exist.

Arnold Zander, founder and first president of AFSCME

The organization is created to promote, defend and enhance the civil service system in Washington state.

The union is the first to be established under AFSCME, but it is named Council 2.

The reason: The Winconsin union became Council 1 out of deference to its favorite son, Arnold Zander.

C.E. Anderson is elected as the first president of Council 2.

1944

An early Council 2 logo.

Seventh annual convention held in Wenatchee

At the seventh annual convention of the Washington State Council, AFSCME, at the Columbian Hotel, Wenatchee, Washington, on July 15, 1944, the union is reported to be growing steadily. Among the local unions represented at the convention are 87, 114, 121, 129, 270, 275, 307, 334, 467, 792 and 827. Members are looking to enlist more members and create more locals.

1950s

Gains achieved in retirement system

LOCAL GOVERNMENT employees are allowed to participate in the Public Employees Retirement System (**PERS**) and Social Security.

Until now, it was not even an option to participate and only the larger jurisdictions have set up their own retirement systems.

1956

State Supreme Court issues key ruling on pension funds

On April 19, 1956, the Washington State Supreme Court issued a significant interpretation on public employee pension funds.

The court ruled that the legal provisions that apply to pensions when public employees start work should remain in force at the time of their retirement, even though the law might have been changed while the person was working.

The case involved H.D. Bakenhus, a retired policeman, and his wife.

Under the law that applied in 1925, Bakenhus was entitled to a pension of $185 a month.

In 1937, however, the law had been amended to provide for a maximum of $125 a month in police pensions. So, when Bakenhus retired, the Police Relief and Pension Fund set his pension at $125 a month.

Bakenhus appealed this ruling, saying he was entitled to the higher pension. The trial court agreed, ruling that the 1937 change in the law did not apply to those who joined the police department before that year.

The City of Seattle appealed the ruling to the Washington State Supreme Court.

The court upheld the trial court ruling. "The respondent has complied with the provisions of his contract," the court ruled.

"He has given twenty-five years of faithful service, during which time he turned down many other opportunities for employment; and, in the meantime, these opportunities necessarily have diminished."

Although the change in 1937 might have introduced other benefits, Bakenhus was entitled to receive the salary under the rules that applied when he joined the police department, the court ruled.

PROFILE

Sam Kinville laid Council 2 foundation

When membership in Council 2 reached 2,000 in 1959, members decided the time had come to appoint a full-time president to handle the growing work.

Until then, the president had served on an unpaid basis.

At the 1959 convention, therefore, members agreed to a resolution changing the constitution to allow for such an appointment and elected Sam Kinville as the first president/executive director.

He was the ideal person for the job, having the union background for which the position called.

Indeed, you could say that Sam Kinville learned to be a union person from the day he was born in Butte, Montana, on March 12, 1926.

The city was so strongly pro-union — it was considered the most unionized city in the United States in those days — that it barred McDonalds from setting up shop there because the fast-food chain was not unionized. The Anaconda Mining Company owned much of the town and most residents were ardent members of the Butte Miners' Union.

Feelings ran so strongly on both sides that Butte experienced strikes

SAM KINVILLE
PRESIDENT 1959–1967

almost every year.

At 17, Kinville went to work for a year in the Anaconda Mining Company's copper mine.

He joined Local Number 1 — and soon learned that the company was "the enemy."

In 1951, Kinville worked in Longview, Washington, as a social worker for the state for a year. During that time he realized that public employees did not have the protection that many union workers for companies did.

He had seen first hand that when workers were unhappy with wages or working conditions they could bring a company to its knees with a prolonged strike.

Using that threat, they could pressure the company into meeting their demands.

"The strike was an economic weapon," Kinville recalled in an interview years later. "But this weapon could not be wielded by those in government service as it was illegal to strike against the government.

"Many questioned the value of unions among public employees; they wondered how public employee unions could bring pressure to bear on their employers."

This situation set Kinville thinking. But it was when he attended the AFSCME convention in the summer of 1956 that he made up his mind what he wanted to do.

He was inspired by Arnold Zander, who, he said, was the opposite of the stereotypical union leader of those days. He had finesse, was a Christian Scientist, had a Ph.D. and was "extremely sophisticated and articulate."

Kinville resigned his job and dedicated himself full-time to the concept that public employees deserved a voice in the decisions on their hours, conditions of employment and wages.

Kinville was appointed a Council 2 staff representative in Spokane. He was one of the first two paid employees of the union.

When he was elected the fourth president of Council 2, and the first to serve full-time, in 1959, Kinville set his sights on obtaining a collective bargaining law in Washington State.

After a long fight, in which Kinville took a leading role, it was passed in 1967.

"That took a lot of effort, but it was certainly worth it," Kinville said. "This is the most significant thing we did.

"It is probably the most important legislation passed in this state concerning the rights of local government employees." (*See Page 16*)

Kinville was also instrumental in the fight for the creation of the Public Employees' Retirement System (PERS) and for the establishment of medical benefits for public employees.

Kinville left Council 2 in 1967 and worked for the Washington State Labor Council for seven years and for the Board of Industrial Insurance Appeals for seven years.

He was named Director of Labor and Industries by Gov. John Spellman in 1981.

He retired in January 1985.

But the next year he returned to Council 2, serving as a contract lobbyist.

In 1994, when he was appointed a member of the Public Employment Relations Commission, he dropped all ties with Council 2 because of concerns about conflict of interest.

Kinville died on September 5, 2005. It was Labor Day — a day he symbolized for many workers. He was 79.

1961

Let's Organize

A stage driver passed o'er a trail one day
Past meadow and woodland he took his way.
His long whip snapped with unerring aim,
Whether standing or moving, 'twas the same.

A horsefly fell as his snaky lash
Shot out, as sure as the lightning's flash,
A grasshopper here and a butterfly there,
Fell prey to his aim as they winged the air.

A hornet's nest hung on a limb nearby,
But the stage driver passed that carefully by.
"What's the matter?" his passenger cried, surprised.
"Why," he answered, "them hornets is organized."

The horsefly, the butterfly, the grasshopper, too
And their fate is a lesson and warning to you.
You will flutter and fall with the hoppers and flies,
Unless, like the hornets, you're organized.

— *County and City Employees NEWS and VIEWS, May 1961*

Legislative office opens in Olympia

The Washington State Council of County and City Employees opened a Legislative Headquarters in Olympia, January 9, 1961.

Plans are for it to stay open during every session of the State Legislature.

The office continues to operate.

1962

THE NEWLY ORGANIZED City of Seattle employees are granted the low number **Local 21** for their charter by AFSCME.

The reason: The local is organized in 1962 during the Seattle World's Fair, the theme of which is Century 21.

1963

Paid medical benefits now possible for families

Until now, the law has allowed counties and cities to pay medical benefits for their employees. Not all do, but some unions have gained such benefits in negotiations.

Legally, however, local governments were not authorized to pay medical and hospitalization plans for employees' spouses and dependents, even should they be prepared to do so.

But with the passage of House Bill 6 in March 1963, counties and cities in Washington State may now pay the total cost of a medical and hospitalization plan for their employees, including spouses and dependents.

Paying them, however, remains a subject for negotiation.

Locals gain employer-paid medical plans

More and more local unions are gaining employer-paid medical benefits. Recent gains:

• Members of **Local 792,** Kittitas County Road Employees, and **Local 367,** Pacific County Road Employees, have received employer-paid medical plans. They were obtained following negotiations between the local unions and county officials.

• Recent negotiations between representatives of **Local 1191,** Walla Walla County Employees, and the Board of County Commissioners have resulted in agreement that the county will pay for the County Road Department employees' share of a group medical plan.

1963

Spokane employees win pay raise

Effective July 1, 1963 Spokane City employees received a long overdue pay raise.

The pay raises ran from $12 to $110 a month, depending on the specific job classification and the individual employee's seniority.

Although all city employees received some wage adjustment, the larger adjustments were granted to the non-uniformed Spokane City employees represented by **Local 270.**

Officers of Local 270 report their membership is encouraged by the City Council's action.

In addition, the union plans to continue to press for a city-paid hospitalization and medical plan.

Many employees say they cannot financially afford to join our union.
The answer is simple, honest and we think sensible:
"It doesn't cost, it pays to belong to our union."
There have been many times that members have gained a benefit worth more than the $4 a month in dues.
They have realized a profit on their $4-a-month investment.

— *County and City Employees NEWS and VIEWS,* January 1963

THAT'LL BE THE DAY!

"I can't accept this raise! The Union won it and I don't belong."

1963

'I'll help you — if you'll help me'

Council 2 had ulterior motives when it supported a bill in the 1963 state legislature granting Washington state county officials pay raises.

It saw the bill as a means to make a significant gain for its members.

Here's how it happened.

Originally, Senate Bill 6 contained only pay raises for state officials. Council 2 supported the bill.

After debating the measure, the Senate reduced the pay raises, but in the House the bill was amended to restore the original pay boosts for elected officials of all 39 counties.

At the urging of Council 2 lobbyists, the House also adopted an amendment that provided for the monthly deduction of union dues from members' pay checks.

This measure was important for Council 2. Although the union had negotiated the payroll deduction of union dues in many counties, officials in some counties had refused to grant this request. The amendment meant they would have to honor it.

Council 2 figured that county officials would not want to oppose a measure that gave them pay raises.

It worked. The bill went back to the Senate where the Senate adopted the House amendments and the bill was passed.

Sam Kinville, left, Council 2 president, discusses the provisions of Senate Bill 6 with Representatives Jack Metcalf (R) and Dick Taylor (D). The two legislators were responsible for the amendment to the bill that provides the right for county employees to have their monthly union dues deducted from their wages.

1963

TESTAMENT TO THE LOSS OF A FRIEND

With the assassination of John Fitzgerald Kennedy, the world lost a leader; the United States lost a president; and we, the officers and members of a labor union for public employees, lost a friend.

World dignitaries will extol his leadership qualities. Prominent citizens of our nation will eulogize his attributes as president. But we alone can testify to his friendship to our precepts.

With his brief appearance on the stage of American history, the whole concept of public service became clearer and even began to shine a bit.

Even if there was disagreement with some of his policies, who could say that he didn't represent the best in courage, intelligence and dedication to public service? Who could say that this man did not add dignity to the concept of public office?

Take the best individuals in the community and employ them for the public good.

Encourage them as public officials; engage them as public employees.

We testify that he not only supported this theory, but did more to advance it than any other before him.

A DELEGATE'S BADGE FOR A FRIEND AT THE RECENT AFL-CIO CONVENTION.

His death was a tragedy, and the tragedy will become indelible if we do not benefit by his example of deeds; if we do not go about our business, as a labor union for public employees, with a renewed vigor, with a firmer determination to improve the lot of the public employee and thereby make our contribution toward improving the public service.

— *County and City Employees NEWS and VIEWS, December 1963*

1964

Bellingham signs labor contract

Another city has signed a collective-bargaining agreement with our union. In November, 1964, the Bellingham City Council signed an agreement with **Local 114,** Bellingham City Employees.

The agreement designates Local 114 as the bargaining agent for all non-uniformed city employees in matters pertaining to hours, wages and conditions of employment. All new employees are required to become union members.

The union's State Council President, Sam Kinville, said collective bargaining agreements between local governments and their organized employees is increasingly becoming the accepted practice. But state law does not provide for collective bargaining and our union's main legislative effort for the coming legislative session will be the passage of such legislation. (*See Page 16*)

1965

Local gains family medical coverage

Effective July 1, 1965, county road department employees of Skagit County who are members of **Local 176** began receiving the benefits of an employer-paid medical and hospitalization plan, negotiated with the Board of County Commissioners.

The officers and members of Local 176 who, until July, had no employer-paid medical and hospitalization plan participated in this major accomplishment from the start.

Several unique features are written in the health and welfare plan:

- The total cost of the plan is paid for by the county;
- The plan covers the employee, spouse and dependents (complete family coverage);
- The maximum cost is $23.60 a month for each individual family.

Insurance proves popular

On November 15, 1965, our State Council began a fourth year of administering a group life insurance program for members of affiliated locals.

When the program was launched in 1961 four locals covering 178 members participated. Now, four years later, 23 locals are taking part covering 1,800 members.

Premiums for the program, which provides a $1,000 death benefit, are $1 a month.

1965

Spokane City in historic agreement

A ground-breaking agreement between the City of Spokane and **Local 270** of the Washington State Council of County and City Employees took effect on January 1, 1965.

It was the first written understanding between an employee group and the City.

The main provisions of the agreement are formal union recognition and a detailed grievance procedure.

Local 270, which represents the non-uniformed City Employees, has long complained about the inadequacy of the Spokane City Civil

Service System. The formal, detailed grievance procedure that is now contained in the union agreement will do much to improve the situation.

Nomination and election of convention delegates

The officers of the following locals in eastern Washington have announced their locals will meet to nominate and elect delegates to the Washington State Council of County and City Employees' Convention to be held in Tacoma Saturday and Sunday, May 22-23, 1965, and the special International Union Convention to be held in Minneapolis, Minnesota, from May 29, 1965.

LOCAL	PLACE	DATE
492, Spokane Sherriffs	Spokane Cnty Courthouse	April 12, 7:30 p.m.
1191, Walla Walla Cnty Rd	Washington Field House	April 13, 8 p.m.
1374 Adams Cnty Rd	WWP Building, Othello	April 8, 8 p.m.
792, Kittitas Cnty Rd	Ellensburg Central Labor	April 9, 8 p.m.
1135, Spokane Cnty Rd	Spokane Cnty Courthouse	April 15, 7:30 p.m.
1553, Spokane Cnty Crthouse	Spokane Cnty Assessors Office	April 20, 7:30 p.m.
270 Spokane City	Water Dept Aud.	April 21, 7:30 p.m.
1254 Lincoln Cnty Rd	Creston Community Hall	April 23, 8 p.m.

1967

Council 2 leads 20-year fight for historic law

Among the game-changing events in the history of Council 2, one stands out above all the others. It was the passing of RCW 41.56 — the Local Government Collective Bargaining Act.

The legislation, passed by the Washington State Legislature in 1967, was to become the road map for almost all the negotiations conducted by Council 2 on behalf of its members.

A dream since the 1940s, it lays the groundwork for Council 2's day-to-day activities and sets forth the rules under which the union and its members work.

Unarguably this Act will benefit the wages, hours and working conditions of all government employees in the future.

"It is probably the most important

Studying the collective bargaining law are Washington State Labor Council President Joe Davis; Council 2 President Sam Kinville; Walt Lambert, Washington State Council of Fire Fighters; and Norm Schut, Washington Federation of State Employees.

legislation passed in this state concerning the rights of local government employees," Sam Kinville, then Council 2 president and a prime mover behind the passing of the law, said.

"Our union led the fight for the collective bargaining rights for local government employees.

"Before that, we had a system of collective begging.

"We would go to a School Board

meeting or a County Commissioner and ask for certain things.

"If they wanted to do so, they gave it to us; if they didn't want to do so, they didn't."

The Act gives workers the guaranteed right by law to form an organization of their own choice and then to meet and negotiate with their employers to discuss hours, wages and conditions of employment.

Once agreement is reached, it is reduced to writing and recorded.

"It ensures workers have a voice in their employment situation," Kinville said. "It marks the death of political patronage."

The goal to secure such a law goes back three decades.

Kinville noted that in the 1930s the Federal Congress passed the National Labor Relations Act. But that law exempted agricultural workers and public employees.

"It was up to the states, if they wanted to do so, to enact their own Act," Kinville said in an interview in 1997.

"Our union was a strong advocate for such a law. Indeed, that was the union's Number One objective."

The passing of the act was not easy. It was realized only after an intense amount of hard work, particularly at the political level, by union leaders who knew what its passage would mean for public employees.

Kinville, who was the Olympia lobbyist for Council 2 as well as president

at the time, spent many, many hours talking to legislators and administration officials.

Hopes were running high in 1964 when the State Senate passed Senate Bill 360 — Collective Bargaining Act for local public employees.

The bill was officially designated as "an act relating to labor relations; authorizing collective bargaining by and between agencies of the state and its political subdivisions and the employees thereof."

'Before that, we had a system of collective begging'

That victory was followed by intensive lobbying in the 1965 session, during which Senate Bill 360 was amended in the House to include public hospital districts.

It passed the House on March 10 by a vote of 62 yes, 35 no, and 2 absent.

The bill was returned to the Senate, and the Senate concurred in the House amendment on the last day of the regular session when the Speaker of the House and the President of the Senate signed the bill on March 11 and sent it to the governor.

In its April 1965 issue, *County and City Employees News and Views* said:

"Our union has been working for 20 years trying to get such a law passed.

"This year the bill was made the number-one priority bill of the United Labor Lobby during the regular legislation session.

"And this year was the year of success as far as the Legislature was concerned."

But Council 2's hopes were short-lived. It turned out that 1965 was not the year of success that the union had hoped it would be.

On March 23, 12 days later, then Governor Dan Evans vetoed the law. On March 31 the Senate attempted to override the governor's veto.

The two-thirds vote required would have been 33 yes. The actual vote was 32 yes and 17 no.

But, over the next couple of years, Kinville and other labor leaders continued to work on the concept and, with the technical assistance of the then director of Labor and Industries in the Evans' administration, Harold Petrie, resubmitted the legislation.

This legislation was subsequently passed and signed by Evans in 1967.

Collective Bargaining remains best answer

As imperfect as our system of bargaining a contract in this state at times can be, it doesn't take too many comparisons to see that it has served us well.

Since 1967, local governments and our membership have hammered out many contracts across the state; in recent years about 280 contracts have been negotiated and settled every three years.

As a result of these agreements our members overall enjoy some of the most competitive wages and benefits in the work force.

Some employers may not wish to admit it, but this is exactly the reason local governments provide the most essential services in the most efficient manner.

In the vast majority of our jurisdictions the collective bargaining process not only has kept the best employees from leaving, but also has created one of the best means of solving day-to-day issues that, if left unresolved, make life unbearable for the employees.

The good employer who wants to please the taxpayer with good services should be as pleased with those gains as our membership.

— *Council 2 President/Executive Director Chris Dugovich*

PROFILE

Larry McKibben built on Kinville foundation

In the wake of Sam Kinville's legislative breakthroughs, Larry McKibben, who served as president for 22 years, continued to consolidate the union as a force to be reckoned with in the ranks of county and city government.

After being elected in 1967, he expanded Council 2's staff, saw a steady rise in membership as a result of significant organizing wins, introduced training sessions for local leaders and boosted the union's lobbying efforts in the Washington State Legislature.

He also set up the annual legislative weekend in Olympia which continues to be an important event on Council 2's calendar.

In 1986 he hired Pamela Bradburn as the union's first general counsel, and welcomed Sam Kinville back in the union's ranks as legislative/political action coordinator. Kinville helped kick Council 2's lobbying efforts back into high gear.

McKibben, who served a term as an AFSCME International vice-president, was regarded as efficient, officials said. He was articulate and knew how to run meetings.

Among McKibben's most challenging times in office were those under

LARRY McKIBBEN
PRESIDENT 1967–1989

the Reagan Administration from 1980 to 1988.

"I am appalled at the political developments in our state and nation this year," he wrote in 1982. "The resulting legislation was a triumph for big business at the expense of labor and most citizens of this state.

"These policies have resulted in nearly 11 million people being out of work, while roads and public services of all kinds continue to deteriorate because of budget cuts and layoffs."

McKibben retired as Council 2 president in 1989.

1970s

How we won against the City of Spokane

When Dean Berry joined **Local 270** as a radio engineer for the City of Spokane, it gave him a sense of belonging to an organization that would help the plight of the poor working man.

"But we didn't have any clout," Berry later recalled. "In those days we had to deal with some pretty harsh realities when talking with the city's bargaining people. It was quite a battle. We had to jawbone them to get anything done, often unsuccessfully.

"Collective bargaining made a big difference. After that, legally, the City had to negotiate with us and could not just ignore our demands. We got good things for the union after the Act became law."

But when he took over as president of Local 270 from John Snell in 1974 Berry was to find out that, even with collective bargaining, sometimes you needed to do more.

At that time the local had an ongoing battle with the City of Spokane over the retirement system. "We had our own

'We made a coffin and took it to City Hall'

retirement system, which allowed for retirement after 25 years of service," Berry said.

Mayor David Rogers adamantly opposed the system. He figured he would lose all the people with 25 years experience, so he wanted everybody to wait until they were 65 to retire, Berry said.

"About 30 or 40 of us picketed City Hall for several days, using our vacation time so that there would not be any comeback.

"One of the guys made a coffin and took it to City Hall. It symbolized the fact that we considered the retirement system to be dead.

"We put it on the sidewalk in front of City Hall, but mostly they carried it around. It was made of cardboard and painted black. The mayor didn't like that at all.

"In time, we got all the retirement system improvements for which we had picketed."

1973

Seattle Public Library union pioneer's slogan was:

'Don't get mad. Organize'

Dissatisfied with low salaries and a campaign of personal innuendo waged by the library administration in the late 1960s, library worker Velma Stanley decided to organize, not get mad.

As a result, she pioneered what later became one of Council 2's largest local unions — that representing staff at the Seattle Public Library.

When Stanley first set about working to establish an AFSCME local union among the classified employees at the library, however, management refused to comply.

Rather than continue on their own, Stanley and her colleagues turned to Council 2's John Malgarini and Tom Bartlett, who successfully helped organize the library clerical workers.

The librarians organized separately, but on February 15, 1973, **Local 2083-N** was born as the representative of the Seattle Public Library's clerical workers.

Elected president of the local, Stanley continued her pioneering work, expanding the local union and leading negotiations with management.

The librarian and clerical workers locals later combined into one

'She was one of our heroes.'

organization, Local 2083.

Stanley continued to work on behalf of her colleagues during the 34 years she worked at the library, devoting decades to improving their lives.

"She was one of our heroes who made our paths so much easier than theirs were," they later said.

"Her experience in confronting management bore fruit for our contract. A strong grievance procedure and language preventing arbitrary promotions were early features of the agreement," colleagues said.

• *Stanley died in December 1997 shortly after she retired at age 60.*

PROFILE

Negotiating was natural to Tony Hazapis

Two talents combined to make Tony Hazapis a natural for negotiating and working in politics.

One was his engaging conversational skills, for which he was famous.

The other was his love for the entertainment industry. A graduate of Gonzaga University, Hazapis served as assistant dean, where he taught a course in entertainment law, before joining Council 2. While serving as Council 2's deputy director from 1980 to 1990, he negotiated the first domestic

TONY HAZAPIS
DEP. DIR. 1980-90

partnership provision in Washington state for the City of Seattle.

He also served as legal counsel for grievance arbitrations and represented King County area locals, including King County Prosecutors.

After leaving Council 2, he represented people who worked for the entertainment industry and was executive director of the Dispute Resolution Center of King County. He was active in Democratic politics.

Hazapis died in 2008.

1982

They said WHAT?

Franklin County Courthouse employees, **Local 874-CH**, could not believe their ears.

During negotiations, County Representative Tony Menke said the county commissioners deserved a higher salary increase than union employees: "Because there have to be Chiefs and there have to be Indians!"

To show how they felt about the insensitive comment, local union employees wore headbands, feathers and badges reading, "I'm a Franklin County Indeon."

(They spelled Indian incorrectly because they did not want to offend Native American citizens.)

Customers, and the local press, smiled — and asked questions.

1983

Local union leads the nation in closing the gender pay gap

The nation's first equal-pay study was initiated by City of Spokane **Local 270** President Jack Miller in 1980, years before it became a hot political issue.

The study was conducted by five city employees appointed by Miller and the city's administrative services manager Gary Persons. They rated each job for supervisory, educational and experience requirements and for its variety and scope of duties. The committee, which found that many employees were underpaid, sent its findings to Miller and Persons.

The City of Spokane cooperated in the study and implemented the findings.

Three years later the findings resulted in pay increases as great as $200 a month for some Spokane City library and clerical staff members, most of them women.

Not only did the study lead to greater gender pay equality, but it also was hailed as a model for public and private organizations to follow.

The story was covered by *Business Week*, which commented in particular on the cooperation between the city and the union in arriving at a solution to pay inequities.

Under the previous salary structure, each position was assigned a pay-range level, Miller told the *Spokesman-Review* in Spokane. "Since the evaluations have been made, some of these positions have been jumped a range or two because their value to the city had been underestimated," he said. "Some have been jumped as much as five levels."

1984

Attorneys first to sign bargaining contract

The **Snohomish County Deputy Prosecutors** have become the first attorneys in Washington to be working under a signed collective bargaining agreement. They are among only a few in the entire nation to do so.

The contract will begin to bring the deputy prosecuting attorneys up to the reasonable rates of pay for which their positions call.

1984

Council 2 wins $1.2 million lawsuit

Snohomish County must pay annual step increases to all qualified employees, a Superior Court judge ruled in a case brought by Council 2.

The lawsuit arose out of a County Council decision in 1983 to freeze the wages of its employees at 1982 levels.

Judge Robert Bibb ruled that the freeze violated the county's own personnel ordinances, which set a five-year step plan that would provide county employees with pay raises as their length of service increased.

"We won for the whole county, not just for us," said the council's General Counsel, Pamela Bradburn.

She noted that Bibb's decision applied to all county employees.

The decision means members will

Chris Dugovich and Pamela Bradburn read announcement of court's decision.

receive retroactive step increases for 1983 and 1984.

When all affected employees are paid, it could cost Snohomish County more than $1.2 million.

Staff Representative Chris Dugovich hailed Judge Bibb's ruling as a major victory for the union, noting that the step increase issue was a stumbling block in contract negotiations, which could now continue.

Oldest member dies

The oldest living member of Council 2, Reinhold Loewe, has died at 93. He became a member in 1937, the year in which Council 2 was founded. An executive board meeting on January 17, 1983, decided to contribute $100 to Second Harvest Food Bank in his memory.

1984

Bringing back Local 270, City of Spokane

The call came to John Cole as he was preparing to attend a New Year's Eve party on the last day of 1983. Council 2 President Larry McKibben was on the line and he had a tough assignment for Cole, who had been a staff representative for four years: Clean up **Local 270**, which was facing allegations of the misuse of funds by its president, who was also a Council 2 staff representative.

John Cole

It was a huge challenge.

"Local 270, which represented employees of the City of Spokane was the largest local in Council 2 at that time," Cole says. "Its 750 members represented a substantial number of our 6,500 employees. Should the local be decertified because of the fraud allegations, we would lose those members, lose a substantial amount of our income, and face an uncertain future.

"It would have been catastrophic."

For nine months, Cole interviewed local members, followed complex paper trails and worked with an audit firm to track where the money had gone. The auditors uncovered the misuse of $40,000. The actual losses probably amounted to as much as $60,000, Cole says.

"Much of the money had been used to buy two racehorses and to pay stable fees."

Cole filed a claim on the union's insurance company and took the evidence to the Spokane County prosecutor. The offender was convicted, paid restitution to the insurance company and spent a brief time in jail.

Some members who had been indirectly involved in the misuse of funds were let go. Intensive training followed. By the end of 1984, the local had been stabilized.

"Joe Cavanaugh took over as the new president and showed strong leadership," Cole adds. "I'm extremely proud of the role he played."

Local 270 became one of the strongest locals in Council 2 and remains such today. (*See Page 56*)

PROFILE

Roy Brannam devoted his life to union causes

R oy Brannam, elected vice president of Council 2 in 1985, was to serve for 18 years, helping to guide the union through challenges and changes, providing valuable advice and help to two presidents.

From his first day in office, Brannam was the ultimate union devotee. When he was not working his day job in the Maintenance and Operations Division of the Clark County Department of Public Services, he was involved in union activities, whether in the evenings, at weekends or on vacation. "To me, going around the state on union business was worth as much as a vacation," Brannam says. "I didn't regret one day of my union involvement."

As the longshoremen's union said in a tribute, "Few people have the drive or desire to invest the time that Roy Brannam dedicated to the union struggle.

"His countless hours of effort and common sense helped us make it through many battles," Council 2 President Chris Dugovich was to recall later. "Over the years, we not only worked well together, but we became good friends. I want to thank him for all his valuable advice and counsel."

Brannam also led **Local 307-CO** in negotiations, and assisted in others.

ROY BRANNAM
VICE PRESIDENT 1985–2003

He says he likes to think he has helped improve people's monetary wellbeing through negotiations he had with counties and cities across the state.

In addition:

• He was chair of the Council 2 Legislative Committee, demonstrating his belief that union members should be politically active.

• He served for 15 years as president of the Central Labor Council of Clark, Skamania & West Klickitat counties, implementing his belief that public employees should work closely with the other unions.

Brannam retired in 2003, but continued to be involved in Council 2 activities.

1986

'How we found a new resource to help us in our negotiations'

The 1986 contract negotiations for **Local 275** in Grays Harbor were long and bitter. But they produced a new resource the local had never used before—the active involvement of the community as well as other unions in the area.

Negotiations began in September 1985. As May approached, it was evident no progress would be made without some kind of action.

As a first step, the union decided to get its dispute in the public eye, said Trina Dempsey, Local 275 chair.

"We asked the public to show their support by signing more than 4,000 letters addressed to the commissioner," she said. "We also wrote 'letters to the editor' to the local newspaper."

A second step was to establish a bond with other unions.

"We supported a strike against Weyerhaeuser in Grays Harbor, walking the picket lines and taking out an ad in the newspaper, forging a new friendship with them."

In turn, other unions supported Local 275. They attended meetings and made hundreds of calls to the commissioners urging them to drop a negotiator they had hired. "Their support kept us going," Dempsey said.

"When we set a September 18 strike deadline, we received offers of help from other unions on our picket lines should we strike.

"We also made our intentions public by renting downtown office space in Montesano and putting up a sign declaring it as our strike headquarters. We put an ad in the paper explaining our position and asked for more public support.

"Then, six days before the deadline, in a mediation session that lasted until 2 a.m., we reached an agreement, a year after negotiations began. Not only was the pressure effective, but our local has become more tightly knit and we have more confidence in ourselves as a team.

"Unions in our area have become more united in their efforts to preserve the quality of life established for labor of all kinds by our unions.

"We saw how effective we can be if we all stick together."

1986

And he wasn't even a union member!

When a Spokane County Corrections Dept. deputy was suspended for five days by Sheriff Larry Erickson in 1986, he wanted to file a grievance against the decision. He considered the action unjust and undeserved.

Randy Withrow

But the deputy — who had refused to join Council 2 because he considered the $6 a month dues on his $552 salary too high — realized he had little chance, as an employee, to argue the case himself. He also knew that provisions for filing a grievance were provided under the collective bargaining agreement.

"So he approached us to represent him," recalled Randy Withrow, a Council 2 staff representative in Spokane from 1980 to 2001.

"We have an obligation to represent even those employees in certain job categories who are not members of the union.

"Under the law we theoretically represent positions covered by the contract, not the individuals."

Council 2 went to court on behalf of the deputy to enforce the collective bargaining contract. The Superior Court for Spokane County ruled in favor of Council 2, but the county appealed. The appeal was turned down by the Appeals Court and the Washington State Supreme Court in July 1986.

"The ruling became effective in all 39 counties," Withrow said. "It was included, for example, in the agreement with Spokane City.

"We went ahead and processed it through the grievance procedure and won that as well for him," Withrow added.

"The deputy continued to work for Spokane County, but still did not join Council 2."

A COUNTY ATTORNEY became so angry during negotiations in the '80s he threw his pencil in the air and it stuck in the ceiling. You could say he left a lasting impression. — *Former Staff Representative Don Boxford.*

PROFILE

Chris Dugovich revitalized Council 2

By 1989 Council 2 was in need of a strong boost. Overall membership growth had slowed, debt was piling up and morale was sagging.

To reinvigorate it, the union elected Chris Dugovich as its new president following the retirement of Larry McKibben. They were not to be disappointed.

Already, Dugovich had made his mark on the union. Armed with a degree in business from the University of Puget Sound, he had joined Council 2 in 1982 as a staff representative in Bellingham. There, he negotiated dozens of contracts, including a number for the City of Bellingham and he presided over the first master agreement for 600 members in Snohomish County.

In 1986, as a deputy director, he had been instrumental in adding members in Snohomish and San Juan counties.

After he was elected president in 1989 — a position he still holds today — Dugovich transformed the union, presiding over gains that saw membership double, turning finances from debt to strong reserves, and boosting morale to a new high.

He achieved these advances by introducing a more business-like approach to Council 2's operations,

CHRIS DUGOVICH
PRESIDENT 1989 – PRESENT

putting members' interests first, and hiring the best staff he could find.

"We became a much more professional operation, doing a better job of representing people," Dugovich says. "We paid our staff salaries that were more comparable with the private sector. We analyzed our budgets. We looked at our situation in a rational manner and we looked at statistics to see what we could learn from them.

"It was not only a matter of boosting morale, but of working more efficiently and more effectively."

To boost membership growth, Dugovich appointed Clem Edwards as the first full-time organizer, a position that Bill Keenan would take up from 1988. Both were highly successful.

Council 2 grew from about 6,500 members when Dugovich took the reins in 1989 to more than 16,000 by 2014, in spite of a falloff as a result of widespread layoffs during the 2007-2009 Great Recession.

The union's debt stood at $200,000 when he took over in 1989. By carefully monitoring spending and boosting income through membership growth, Dugovich soon eliminated the debt and built up the reserves.

In 1992, under his direction, Council 2 purchased its own headquarters building in Everett (*see Page 42*), later gaining additional income through rentals. The purchase of buildings in Spokane in 1996 and Olympia in 2007 followed. The buildings represent a significant investment.

Above all, Dugovich placed a premium on seeing to members' interests.

• He ensured that members received expert help at the negotiating table and when they filed grievances against management.

• As far as possible he fostered good relationships with management, knowing that this would achieve more success than blunt confrontation.

• He kept alive and grew the Health and Welfare Trust, set up in the mid-70s, that provides benefits at a reasonable cost. (*See Page 48*)

• In 1990, he introduced a scholarship program in recognition of the valuable role the union could play in helping members' families cover higher education costs.

The first scholarships were modest (*see Page 31*), but in future years, as college costs steadily rose, they were increased and totaled $86,000 in 2014.

• He introduced an annual golf tournament that helped boost the scholarship fund. The 2014 tournament, held at Chambers Bay in Pierce County, raised $24,250.

• He showed strong support for the Women's Committee, encouraging it to be increasingly active within the union. (*See Page 49*)

Among the highlights of his presidency, Dugovich says, have been:

• The strikes in 1991 in Mason County (*see Page 31*);
• The Spokane jail strike, the courthouse strike that followed in June 1992 (*see Pages 35 and 36*); and
• The Renton strike in November 1992 (*see Page 39*).

"The strikes got us much media play across the state," he says. "All were membership driven. They were largely disputes over medical benefits, which remains a problem today."

In 1996 Dugovich was elected from the Northwest Region (Alaska, Oregon, Washington, Idaho, Montana) of AFSCME to the position of International Vice President. He was re-elected in 2000 and served until 2004. The position serves on AFSCME's International Executive Board.

1990

Mason County courthouse employees stage 7-day strike

Intransigence by Mason County management forced a seven-day walkout by county courthouse employees in late April, 1990, but the perseverance of the 36 members of **Local 1504** paid off in the form of a reasonable contract settlement.

Council 2 union locals rallied behind the Mason County employees, chipping in money to help compensate them for seven days' lost wages.

Council 2 President Chris Dugovich said management's proposals for wages and medical benefits were "ridiculously low."

Mason County courthouse employees seek community support.

"No one ever wants to strike except as a last resort, but management's hardline stance left Local 1504 members with no other option," Dugovich said.

The settlement was unanimously ratified.

THE FIRST COUNCIL 2 SCHOLARSHIPS were awarded in 1990 when Carrie Crowell, 17, daughter of Local 114 member Shirley Knapp, and Alan Krebs, 34, son of Local 1191 member Crystal Krebs, each received a $1,000 grant from Council 2.

President/Executive Director Chris Dugovich said the council leadership initiated the scholarship program in recognition of the valuable role the union could play in helping members' families cover higher education costs.

"We realize college costs are not getting any less expensive," Dugovich says. "We're pleased we're able to do this to help out."

1990

They toiled for two long months to save a local union

It looked disastrous.

City of Yakima members of **Local 1122** had filed a petition to decertify Council 2. If it were to be ratified by the employees, the move would mean that the union would lose 380 members, a large chunk of the 7,500 or so members that the union had at the time.

Joe Parisi

The petition had been signed by 250 employees. If they all voted in favor, that would be more than enough to ensure passage. Something had to be done. And done quickly ahead of the December vote.

Council 2 President Chris Dugovich dis-

Clem Edwards

patched Clem Edwards, then Council 2 Organizing Director, to Yakima. He also sent the best union fixer-upper he knew — Joe Parisi, who worked for AFSCME.

"Joe always had a sort-of street smart rule for dealing with any situation and how people should be treated," Dugovich recalls. He used to compare his job as an area director for AFSCME with that of a paratrooper. "Ya know, Chris, I drop in, fix the problem, and get out."

Parisi and Edwards booked into a local hotel. They were to stay for two long grueling months in which they attempted to contact every local member to persuade them to stay in Council 2.

Dugovich would visit often to assist them.

"We met with the people at their work sites," Edwards recalls. "For example, we got up at 4 a.m. to meet the garbage disposal workers when they began their shift at 5 a.m. We listened to their problems. We told them what Council 2 would do for them.

"They believed us."

When the vote was held, the decertification petition was rejected by a landslide.

Disaster averted.

1990

LUCK OF THE IRISH

Sometimes it is better to be lucky than good in negotiating. So says **Local 270** President Joe Cavanaugh.

To illustrate his point, he tells the story of the time in early 1990 when Spokane City employees blanketed City Hall with an endless line of pickets. The members of Local 270 had worked for months without a contract, negotiations were going nowhere, and they wanted to vent their frustration.

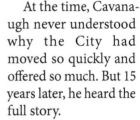

"Suddenly, one day I had a call from the City negotiator," recalls Cavanaugh. "He asked to meet with me about 10 a.m.

"When we met, he came with a proposal that was better than the one we had made earlier in the negotiations.

"I was amazed. We called off the picketing. We ratified a new contract in a few days."

At the time, Cavanaugh never understood why the City had moved so quickly and offered so much. But 15 years later, he heard the full story.

"A delegation from Limerick, Ireland was coincidentally due in Spokane that afternoon," he says. "Apparently the mayor, Shari Barnard, had gone to the city negotiators and said, 'If I see one picket outside City Hall this afternoon, you'll both be looking for a job.'

"We knew she was a friend of labor. We just didn't know how good."

DURING A HEATED dues debate at the 1991 Everett Council 2 Convention President Chris Dugovich recognized Willie Stowers, who was waiting to speak, as Willie Nelson. His response was a short rendition of "On The Road Again."

PROFILE

Judy Johnson reshaped the union's finances

Y ou could say that in 1991 Judy Johnson, an employee in the Bellingham Police Department, began policing Council 2's financial records. And for 16 years she did so with the diligence, attention to detail and integrity demanded of every police officer.

Johnson served for almost 10 years as secretary-treasurer and later president of **Local 114** before being appointed secretary-treasurer for Council 2. Following the mandate of the then new President Chris Dugovich, she oversaw the complete financial restructuring of the union.

When she took over the position — which oversees all the financial record keeping and provides key checks and balances to the union — Council 2 had fewer than 7,000 members and was running a financial deficit. When she retired in 2007 it was a financially strong

JUDY JOHNSON
SECRETARY-TREASURER
1991–2007

16,000-member union.

Johnson was praised for her long service to the union, at both the local and executive level, her attention to detail, and the can-do spirit she brought to all her roles in the union.

FOR 18 YEARS, at every convention, **John E. Walker,** the official convention photographer, snapped everything that went on. He climbed a small stepladder to get a better view. He called out instructions to those on the podium. He twisted and turned to get the best picture. When he retired in 2007 he had become a convention trademark. "The good, well-intentioned people of Council 2 made it all worthwhile," he said.

1992

One-day strike leads to big win — and law change

Correctional officers went on strike in March, 1992 for the first time in Washington state history. It would also be the last time correctional officers in the state would go out on strike.

More than 100 Spokane County correctional officers and members of **Local 492** walked off the job after then Local President Mike Smith called a meeting of all the local members on a Friday evening.

"I said negotiations have gone as far as we have been able to go," he recalls. I want you to give me strike authorization."

"A member asked, 'When do you want us to go on strike?'

"I said, 'How about midnight tonight?'

"They agreed."

With the officers on strike and deputies called off the street to fill jobs that few of them knew anything about, negotiations with the county resumed at 7 p.m. Saturday.

By 9 p.m. the county had moved from a 2 percent offer to an offer of 8 percent increases over nine months.

In a short time, a tentative agreement had been reached.

The correctional officers returned to work on Sunday, March 8.

The strike had an effective by-product as a result of action by Smith that effectively prevented a similar strike from taking place again.

"I networked with other jails and drafted a bill to give to the State Legislature," Smith recalls.

"That bill would provide correctional officers throughout the state with interest arbitration, meaning

'In short time, agreement had been reached'

that they would not have to go on strike again for wages."

Assisted by Sam Kinville, then a lobbyist in Olympia for Council 2, Smith persuaded a state legislator to sponsor the bill, after which he spent three days talking to legislators in Olympia about the measure.

It passed unanimously.

"It put correctional officers on the same footing as police and firefighters," Smith adds.

1993

Council 2 President Chris Dugovich addresses strikers.

Spokane County walkout is ...

Washington's largest public employees strike

A strike by **Local 1553** shut down the Spokane County court system for six days in June, 1993.

The action by the local, which consists mostly of clerical and technical staff in Spokane County Courthouse, is believed to be the largest public employees strike ever to take place in Washington state. At one stage some 1,300 members of Local 1553 and their supporters were on the picket lines.

The spark for the strike, called after bargaining broke down between the local and the Spokane County Administration, was a resolution passed by the county commissioners that would have given non-union workers a larger pay increase than union members.

But a long history of conflict lay behind the strike, said Council 2 President Chris Dugovich.

"This thing had been building for more than 10 years because of a lack of respect from the county for the union and its members," he said. "They were late for meetings, they didn't put proposals in writing and the people had had enough. It was a lack of common courtesy on their part."

Pickets went up as early as 3 a.m. on Wednesday, June 9.

The line was not only honored by all the other unions in the building, but also by 500 others who were not even members of a union.

In addition, the courthouse workers set up pickets outside the Spokane County Jail.

When they arrived for work, 125 correctional officers refused to cross the picket line. They did not go home, but stood outside the building.

"We had a contract that we could not go on strike," Mike Smith, who was then president of **Local 492**

(Spokane County Corrections), says. "But we refused to cross the picket line.

"We were videotaped and threatened by deputies who told us we

Council 2 President Chris Dugovich answers questions from TV reporters. The strike received significant media coverage.

would be disciplined and might even lose our jobs," Smith says. "We knew that they could not simply fire all of us as there would then be no one to run the jail.

"I suggested the courthouse employees picket the jail all the time, and not just from 8 a.m. to 5 p.m.," says Smith,

"That way they would effectively stop officers from going to work when they arrived for their early-morning and late-night shifts."

The result: Spokane County government effectively stopped working in the courthouse and also at the jail.

A festive mood developed among the correctional officers, who held cookouts and sing-a-longs, made lunch, and just sat outside.

Meantime, the courthouse employees continued their picketing. Soon the pressure began mounting on Spokane County officials in the face of a united union front.

As the strike continued into its third day on Friday, county officials agreed to attend a bargaining session.

After 12 hours of negotiation at the weekend, agreement was reached on pay increases of 3 percent and 100 percent of the Seattle-Tacoma cost-of-living index.

The workers returned to their duties June 15 and the resolution giving non-union workers higher increases was rescinded.

STRIKE SIDELIGHTS

Dean Vercruysse, Council 2 staff representative at the time, remembers:

☐ Jail Lieutenant Edie Hunt looking over the top floor of the Spokane Jail down on the strikers below and Council 2 staffer Bill Keenan yelling up to her, "Don't jump, it's not worth it."

***

☐ Jail Sergeant Mike Rohrscheib being caught on TV giving strikers the one-fingered salute.

***

☐ A TV news reporter filming the Sheriff Department's Public Information Officer filming the strikers.

***

Council 2 President Chris Dugovich recalls:

☐ A striking member told me his wife had attempted to file divorce papers during the strike, but was unable to do so because the courts were closed as a result of the strike. Council 2 does save families.

1993

Boeing workers help Renton strikers to reach settlement

About 280 Renton City members of **Local 21-R**, walked off the job November 9, 1993 after negotiations with the city had been going on for nearly a year with little resolution in sight.

During this time management had received huge pay increases. They stayed off for two weeks before the City Council finally approved more money to meet their demands.

The strike shut down many city operations, including the municipal court, building

Dee Maine poses with the Thanksgiving turkey she and other strikers received.

inspections and permits, Maplewood Golf Course and all financial and clerical work in City Hall.

During the walk-off, the Renton workers received a strong assist from workers at the Longacres Boeing office complex.

In a show of solidarity, union building trades workers on the 757 project walked off the job, halting work on the project for a day. The Renton strike was settled the following day.

The next day the Renton City workers were back on the job.

A MAINTENANCE WORKER for a small city in Washington State was found to be positive in a marijuana test, former Staff Representative Dean Vercruysse recalls. When challenged, he claimed he had eaten two brownies at a holiday party and didn't know they had any drugs in them.

When the City Manager saw the test results he declared, "Judging by the concentration of marijuana in his system, the guy would have died of chocolate poisoning if he had eaten that many brownies."

PROFILE

Mike Smith: Active at all levels

Mike Smith has seen many unions at work across the United States, particularly in the field of corrections. He rates Council 2 at the top.

As a staff representative for Council 2 for 16 years, he oversaw 25 contracts in Eastern Washington for the union, and served on the International Corrections Advisory Committee from 1995 to 2012, helping set policy for AFSCME on corrections issues. He also was a member of the national Corrections and Criminal Justice Committee for five years.

"When you look at others, our union is probably the most progressive and well managed of all," he says. "It is head and shoulders above everything that is out there. I am very proud to have worked for Council 2."

Smith first became involved in Council 2's **Local 492** in 1982 when he began work as a correctional officer in the Spokane County Jail. He soon was elected local president.

"I regarded being a Council 2 member as a fundamental necessity for a better life in terms of wages, working conditions — everything," he says. "Council 2, and specifically Chris Dugovich, supported us wholeheartedly in all of our efforts and was instrumental in negotiating

MIKE SMITH
STAFF REPRESENTATIVE
1997–2013

settlements to our issues. "At first, working conditions were pretty miserable; now they're pretty good."

When he retired as a corrections officer in 1997, he joined Council 2 full-time, representing corrections officers in locals across Eastern Washington where he brought his extensive knowledge and experience to bear.

In addition, for 10 years he primarily represented the City of Spokane, largest local union in Council 2.

He retired at the end of 2013, but in 2015 was still working part-time for Council 2.

1994

Worker succeeds in having highway law changed

During Council 2's 1994 legislative weekend, Roger Moller, secretary-treasurer of **Local 109**, checked out bills being considered by the state legislature.

He noticed Senate Bill 5995 would beef up penalties for drivers who disregarded the safety of workers in highway construction zones. But Moller, whose local represents the **Snohomish County road crew,** suggested the bill be amended to refer to all roadways and not only

Roger Moller

highways.

Council 2's Olympia lobbyist Sam Kinville spoke with State Sen. Larry Vognild, who changed the wording and moved the measure through the senate.

Pat Thompson, staff representative in Council 2's head office, thanked Moller for using his initiative to bring about an important change in state law. "This might seem a small change, but the ramifications were great," he said.

Bad evaluations are destroyed

The City of Spokane destroyed and rewrote at least 54 error-filled performance evaluations as a result of a grievance filed by Council 2.

The evaluations illegally cited on-the-job injuries and use of sick leave. Additional errors included evaluations completed by the wrong supervisor and performed after fewer than 60 days of supervision.

Eighth office is opened

On March 1, 1993, Council 2 opened its eighth office — in Wenatchee — that will enhance its accessibility to the North Central Washington area. With this latest opening, the union boasts offices on the east side in Spokane, Pasco, Yakima and Wenatchee.

RAINIER BUILDING CORPORATION

Building purchases deliver a great financial success story

In 1994 the union was growing quickly and needed space for a larger staff. Instead of renting additional space, Council 2 decided to buy its own building, creating the Rainier Building Corporation to do so. The union's leadership reckoned it made sense to invest in a building for the same reasons it makes sense to buy rather than rent your own home.

Everett building when it was bought in 1996.

Over the next 12 years the union invested in buildings in Spokane and Olympia in addition to Everett.

The moves proved to be an outstanding financial success story for Council 2.

Here's a look at each purchase.

• In 1996, the union bought a building in Everett that had been built in the early 80s by the Howard S. Wright construction company to house the Anderson Hunter law firm.

The union bought the building for $825,000, with a down payment of $250,000. Financing was secured through Frontier Bank, a sizable player in the local area.

For the first 18 months Council 2 leased the building back to the law firm until their new space was completed. Staff moved into the building in early 1996.

The purchase has been a great investment. Rental receipts paid for the much-needed remodel and clean-up (about $80,000). When interest rates dropped, Council 2 refinanced; the building was then valued at $1.2 million.

• In the fall of 1995 Council 2 bought its Spokane building on West Francis in North Spokane for $550,000. The purchase included an adjacent sizable lot with two aging and unusable foundations. The building came with three tenants, who ensured a positive cash flow from day one, and an unfinished space on the first floor, which the union refurbished and occupied in 1996. Financing was provided by Tacoma's TAPCO Credit Union.

Over the years many improvements were made to the Spokane building, which included replacing the old foundations next door with a sizable parking lot. Council 2's staff later moved upstairs.

In 2000 the union sold the adjacent lot — originally valued at $50,000 — for $160,000 to a local credit union for the construction of a new branch. The credit union later sold the lot to a Spokane landowner.

• In August 2006 the union bought its third building, on Olympia's west side, close to the Thurston County Courthouse, at a cost of $720,000 and an additional $120,000 needed to refurbish the interior.

At the same time Council 2 changed the building corporation's structure to allow individual investors. In this way it avoided a portion of the additional debt by allowing investors to share in the profit of the corporation through the payment of dividends.

Eight individuals and entities (mainly local unions in Council 2) collectively bought 5.5 percent of the corporation.

• In 2014 the building corporation purchased the vacant lot next to the Everett building for $160,000 as a possible site for a future building.

The three buildings that make up The Rainier Building Corporation have been a real success story financially for the union. Additionally, they have provided needed space for staff along with meeting space for local union meetings.

They also have shown employers that Council 2 has real resources and will be here for many years. A force to be reckoned with! As a symbol, therefore, they are all-important.

• In the five years to 2015, the corporation has paid out dividends of more than $500,000. Of those, 94.5 percent have been paid to the union. That's why, even during the 2008-2010 recession, Council 2 was able to maintain its services without going to its membership for a dues increase during the toughest of times.

Together the buildings have all increased in value.

COUNCIL 2's SALE of a lot adjacent to its Spokane property to a credit union in 2000 seemed a great match for Council 2, but the credit union later sold the property to a conservative landowner in Spokane. A result: During the political season, the prime location often displays candidate's signs whose views the union does not share.

1996

Breaking the state barrier

In 1996, workers in Coeur d'Alene, Idaho, became the first outside Washington state to join Council 2.

They were not new to unions, having organized themselves in 1981 under the Service Employees International Union (SEIU). Also, even though Idaho was a right-to-work state, they had won collective bargaining rights for their union in 1981.

The new members were 80 Lake City employees — streets, parks, water, clerical and other workers who, on joining Council 2, became **Local 433**.

With them came ardent union leaders who had worked tirelessly to bring workers' rights to their part of Idaho.

Among them were Bill Keenan, who became Council 2's first staff representative in Spokane and later Organizing Director; Robin Ricks, president of Local 433 who worked for the Coeur d'Alene Water Department and later served on Council 2's executive board; and Bill Head.

"We preferred to join AFSCME as it represented only local government workers and SEIU represented largely private company workers," Keenan explained.

The leaders not only had brought unions to Idaho, they also had demonstrated their ability to achieve union gains in innovative ways.

To gain collective bargaining rights, they had helped develop a highly unusual plan with an unlikely coalition of four groups with widely differing interests: The City employees, the Coeur d'Alene Fire Fighters Union, the Kootenai Environmental Alliance and a Coeur d'Alene senior citizens group.

The plan called on the voters to support the endorsed three council member candidates and the endorsed mayoral candidate as a group.

By voting in the three candidates and the mayor they would ensure a majority on the council, which consisted of six members and the mayor.

The plan also called on the four elected officials to sign a pledge that, once elected, they would:

• Reinstate the fire fighters, who had been fired for going on strike.

• Pass a shore-line protection ordinance prohibiting the construction of high-rise buildings along the shores of Lake Coeur d'Alene.

Robin Ricks

• Develop a new senior center, which the council had failed to do for years.

• Grant city employees collective bargaining rights through a city ordinance.

Each of the groups in the coalition had a favorite cause. On their own, each might experience headway, but as a group they could all win.

Of course, for the Lake City employees, having collective bargaining rights would be the reward for supporting the other causes.

During the campaign, yard signs bore four names. Vote for them all, the coalition urged, or none at all.

The result was the largest voter turnout in the history of Coeur d'Alene at that time.

The package deal formula proved to be a great success.

"After winning the election, the mayor, assisted by the three labor-friendly council members, kept their part of the agreement and helped us gain a collective bargaining ordinance for the City," Ricks recalled.

"Our goal, which we achieved, was the unionization, not just of a few departments, but of all the city's employees.

"We felt we would have more power if all the employees could negotiate for a fair living wage, benefits and working conditions."

The victory set them up as highly suitable candidates for Council 2 membership, Ricks says.

"We were the lions at the gate.

"Needs change, mayors and councils come and go, employees retire, but the contract and collective bargaining stand."

But, 17 years after the 1981 victory, and two years after the members had joined Council 2, new office bearers came into office and collective bargaining was removed.

This time, Council 2 would be called upon to ensure the workers' rights were regained.

And they would be called upon to show an innovative approach, just as the leaders of Local 433 had done before.

To find out how they did it see Page 51.

1997

This time, talking wins

Chalk up a victory for peaceful negotiations.

After three years of hard work, a new contract has been signed between **Local 21-R** and the City of Renton.

The successful negotiations came in the wake of a bitter strike three years ago which lasted for two weeks, and shut down many aspects of city operations. (*See Page 39.*)

From then, Local 21-R, assisted by Council 2 Staff Representative Kathi Oglesby, worked hard to try to prevent a repeat of the climate that led to the strike and the strike itself. At the same time, the local was committed to making gains in its contract.

They accomplished both goals when the Renton City Council, which clearly did not want another strike, approved more money to meet the workers' demands.

Appraisers to get $50,000 in back pay

Five Spokane County appraisers could jointly receive $50,000 in back pay following an arbitrator's ruling.

Arbitrator Howell L. Lankford agreed with the argument by Audrey Eide, general counsel for Council 2, that Spokane County breached a settlement agreement with **Local 1553** by paying appraisers working at the level of Appraiser 3 at the level of Appraiser 2.

The back pay extends back nearly three years.

Michealanne O'Neill, union member and steward, whose record keeping and testimony were critical to the success of the appraisers' case at arbitration.

Commissioner 'wrong to have negotiated directly'

The Public Employment Relations Commission has ruled that a Benton County commissioner committed an unfair labor practice by negotiating directly with bargaining unit employees.

The commissioner's comments to members were seen as denigrating the union, PERC ruled.

Council 2's General Counsel Audrey Eide argued the action was discrimination against the union.

PROFILE

Audrey Eide charts union's legal waters

When language in contract negotiations gets complex, a grievance hearing turns sour or an unfair labor practice needs to be filed, Council 2 members turn to a reliable source for information, guidance and action. That source is Audrey Eide, the union's full-time general counsel since 1993.

"She'll sort out the complex legal side," members say. "We know she will." And she does.

After graduating from the University of Washington with a bachelor's degree in business, Eide earned a law degree, that of Juris Doctor, at the University of Puget Sound's Tacoma law school. She worked as general counsel at the Washington Public Employees Association, a small labor union that represented state employees.

In 1991 she joined Council 2 on a part-time basis. Two years later she was named general counsel.

Over the years she has represented Council 2 in arbitrations, enforcing languages in contracts, filing unfair labor practices, and other legal disputes. (*See Pages 46 and 53.*)

Eide has not kept count of how many cases in which she has represented Council 2, but they are numerous. "We administer more than

AUDREY EIDE
GENERAL COUNSEL
1993–PRESENT

200 contracts," she explains.

"The staff representatives handle grievances or disputes over contracts to the arbitration level. I determine whether we should go forward. If we do, I represent the union in the hearing."

Eide has found union work to be a perfect match for her.

"Labor law suits my liberal philosophy," she says. "It is a purposeful career and I feel good about what I do. I love being on the union side.

"It is rewarding to obtain remedies beneficial to union members, such as when I secure reinstatement for someone wrongfully treated or terminated."

HEALTH AND WELFARE TRUST

Beating the big guys

SINCE 1976, Council 2's Health and Welfare Trust has provided dental, vision, long-term disability and life-insurance benefits to those members who participate on a group basis.

When given the opportunity, the trust has almost always beaten out the cost effectiveness of plans offered by the nationwide insurance companies, in spite of their huge marketing abilities.

The program has proven popular. By 2015, more than 3,500 Council 2 members participated in the trust, which seeks to provide the best benefits at the lowest cost.

Fourteen dental plans make up the largest component.

In 2015, the trustees, made up of union officers, were President Chris Dugovich, Vice-President Ron Fredin and Secretary Treasurer Kathleen Etheredge.

To gain the benefits of the trust, members should:

- Present a proposal to the employers to be covered by one of the plans and in the next contract negotiations bargain that the employer pays the premium, or

- By majority vote, the local union can choose to participate and add the premium to the monthly dues.

1997

GENERAL ELECTION HELPS PREVENT STRIKE

AN APPROACHING general election helped avert a strike planned by 244 members of **Local 1308 i**n Kitsap County for November 3, 1997.

County management was clearly aware that if a strike had taken place it would have severely disrupted the November 4 elections in Kitsap County as the union represented nearly all the county election staff.

Tentative agreement on a three-year contract was reached an hour before employees were ready to walk out. The election went ahead as planned.

PROFILE

Lois Clement: 'Godmother of Council 2'

For most people, retiring means, well, retiring. But for Lois Clement it meant a new burst of energy.

In 1997, when she retired from the Bellingham Public Library, where she had worked for 31 years, she could have stepped down from active involvement in Council 2 as well. After all, as a leader in **Local 114**, which represents workers at the Bellingham Public Library, she had helped achieve significant gains for the staff over many years.

But she volunteered to take over the reins of the Women's Advisory Committee after pioneering women's leader Mary Hersey died in 1997.

Encouraged by Council 2 President Chris Dugovich, who strongly supported the committee, she set about expanding the group.

In addition to a women's breakfast at conventions, she introduced workshops and luncheon meetings for women on the executive board.

She played a leading role in choosing the winners for the Hersey Awards (*see Pages 97–102*), named in honor of the former women's leader.

"I worked mostly to encourage women to be involved," she said. "I didn't want our women to put themselves down."

LOIS CLEMENT
WOMEN'S LEADER
1997–2011

After inviting outside women to speak at events, she suggested that Council 2 women themselves address the workshops in the future. "Our women became comfortable in taking part," she added.

For a time Clement also worked with the Washington State International Women's Committee.

"She is considered to be the godmother of Council 2," Lee Saunders, Secretary-Treasurer of AFSCME, said during a convention speech when Clement stood down from the union in 2011. "She has been committed and dedicated to this union for many years."

1998

They went, they saw, they participated

I t was grassroots lobbying at its best. When more than 150 Council 2 members took part in the annual Legislative Weekend in late January, they did more than simply meet legislators.

They actively lobbied the lawmakers to discourage them from passing the latest amendments to state retirement bills. They went armed with letters outlining Council 2's objections to the latest pension bills. They met with senators and representatives to express their frustration with a system that takes their money, but shuts them out of the policy-making process.

This year's Legislative Weekend was the biggest to date. It continues to grow in popularity.

"People are really enjoying the ability to meet with their legislators, to discuss the issues that are important to them," says Council 2's Legislation/Political Action Director Pat Thompson.

Similar successful Legislative Weekends have been held every year since 1988.

WHEN COUNCIL 2 first represented **Local 433** in Coeur d'Alene, Idaho, in the late 90s, the City did not recognize the union, telling Staff Representative Bill Keenan he had to sit outside during negotiations. Members of the local's negotiating team had to leave the room to ask him questions.

It was, recalls Local 433's Robin Ricks, like having the bus driver sit outside the bus and try to drive it by remote control.

Later when Staff Representative Gordon Smith took over, anti-union sentiment had thawed a little and he was permitted to be in the room, but was not allowed to sit at the table and was not permitted to speak.

After Council 2 protested several times, the City consulted its attorney who explained the union's representative was entitled not only to be present, but also to lead the discussions. Smith was then given a seat at the table as the primary spokesperson.

1999

'Tremendous victory' in Coeur d'Alene, Idaho

The horse trailer being towed along I-90 contained an unusual load: 500 signs.

They were destined for Coeur d'Alene where they would be a weapon in a determined drive to win an initiative. Victory would restore collective bargaining rights for Coeur

Paula Payne, President of Local 433 (front, third from left) with local members who helped ensure a resounding victory in Initiative 1 in Coeur d'Alene.

d'Alene City workers granted in 1981 (*see Page 44*), but recently removed by the City Council. Now Council 2 was hoping to give more permanence to the rights through an initiative that could not be easily removed.

After an all-night ride, Pat Thompson, Council 2's Legislation/Political Action Director, parked the trailer at the Union hall. Thirty eager members were waiting to plant the signs in yards, businesses and other sites around town, as were newly appointed staff representative Gordon Smith and Robin Ricks, who was on hand from Coeur d'Alene.

Also on hand was a snow storm. But, undeterred by the weather, the workers completed their task in three days. On the morning of the Feb. 2 election, 50 of the local members were at the hall to collect signs to wave at strategic points around town. They faced another snow storm. Conditions were as bad as they could get.

But the storm gave the citizens of Coeur d'Alene an example of how vital the City employees were. They were plowing streets, clearing the roads of fallen trees, and restoring power.

The dedication and determination — both to the job and to the cause — paid off. A total of 59 percent voted in favor of the initiative.

Collective bargaining rights were restored.

1999

Copy of Council 2 newspaper, *County & City Employee* featuring an article on a telephone call by Vice President Al Gore during the 1999 convention. At the top is a note signed by the vice president thanking Council 2 President Chris Dugovich.

DURING A STRIKE Council 2 President Chris Dugovich walked into the negotiating room to see the nine members of the bargaining team pressing their ears against the wall, some with drinking glasses, trying to hear what management was saying in the next room.

***

Then there was the elected official who used to slip out of the bargaining sessions for a quick nip of his favorite beverage.

***

A tipsy lady barged into a late-night bargaining session at a hotel and commenced to call several elected officials and the union negotiating team boring and invited them to the lounge to dance.

2000

Ruling on comparables is breakthrough for union

Council 2 won a major victory for its members in an arbitration hearing in Spokane.

The hearing—on issues in contract negotiations between **Local 492**, (correction officers), and Spokane County—involved "comparables," or the way in which wages are determined by comparing them with other counties or areas.

Arbitrator Gary Axion found that larger counties in Western Washington can be used as comparisons on wages and other issues for Spokane County rather than the inclusion of smaller Eastern Washington counties, which was an earlier precedent.

Members of Local 492 (Spokane County) smile after hearing the arbitration ruling on comparables. They are (from left) Ken Erickson, Tom Trarbough, Ken Thomas and Jay Shuman. In the center at the back is Staff Representative Gordon Smith.

The union believes the ruling provides a guideline that can be used in future negotiations.

Senior Counsel Audrey Eide represented Council 2 at the hearing.

Here's an answer to contracting-out

If you can't beat them, join them. That was the approach taken by Council 2 when Clark County contracted out its counseling services.

After meeting with Council 2 officials, the 170 mental health professionals from the two contracting companies voted 80 percent in favor of joining Council 2, bringing them under similar collective bargaining benefits and wages and salary structures as those enjoyed by Council 2 members

"If they are going to contract out the work to private-sector companies, we are going to go get them," says Council 2 Organizer Bill Keenan.

2000

New pension policy is a major victory for members

Finally, all the lobbying, the serving on committees and the sheer determination paid off.

Passage of a new pension policy approved unanimously in both houses during the 2000 legislative session was a fitting reward for Council 2's constant involvement and persistent pressure on the Joint Committee on Pension Policy.

The new law lowers the penalty from 40 percent to 15 percent for those retiring at age 60 rather than 65 with 30 years' service.

Members, such as correctional officers, believe a retirement age of 65 is impractical for those who daily perform physically-demanding work.

"Like most pension improvements, we won't see the benefit of this immediately," Pat Thompson, Director of Legislation/Political Action for Council 2, says. "But many now in their 30s and 40s will recognize this as a major benefit when they are 60."

Thompson, who served as chair of the Public Employees Pension Coalition, says that Council 2 refused to

yield throughout the years of negotiation. "We hung tough," he says. "Other employee organizations caved, but we and the other AFL-CIO unions did not. The result was that we won in the end. It proves that perseverance and being true to your principles pays off."

This legislation was improved even more in 2007 (see Page 64).

Deputy prosecutors get their rights back

Council 2 achieved a significant victory with the bipartisan passage in a tied state legislature of Senate Bill 5152 granting deputy prosecutors collective bargaining rights.

Their rights were stripped away in 1994 by the state Supreme Court in a 5-4 decision. "We decided to work to legislatively overturn the court decision," said Pat Thompson, Director of Legislation/Political Action. "We succeeded. It was a big plus for us."

2001

Public employee heroes were among attack victims

The world changed on September 11, 2001 and we all changed with it.

In the initial shock of the vicious attacks in New York and Washington D.C., our thoughts went out to the victims and their families, AFSCME, through its affiliates, CSEA and District Council 37, which represent the New York State employees and the City of New York employees.

Losses occurred to emergency personnel who responded to the scene and were caught up in the tragedy. Father Mychal Judge, the New York Fire Department chaplain, and member of AFSCME Local 299, as well as Carlos Lillo and Ricardo Quinn, emergency medical technicians and members of Local 2507, were lost at the World Trade Center.

These public employee heroes, along with countless friends, neighbors and relatives of AFSCME members, are now gone.

AFSCME has set up a disaster relief fund to aid the families of those lost. Council 2's Executive Board made a sizable contribution. If your local union wishes to assist in this effort you can make out your check to Council 2 and we will forward it to AFSCME.

— *Chris Dugovich, Council 2 President and Executive Director.*

Contracts approved at a rapid pace

Council 2 bargaining units ratified more than 100 contracts during 2001, making the year one of the busiest ever for Council 2 negotiations. One contract was approved about every 2½ working days.

The number reflects the uncertainty of the times in public agencies, rising medical insurance costs, and the hard work of Council 2 staff representatives to complete negotiations in a timely manner.

Local unions renewed bargaining contracts, settled some pending for years, and negotiated new ones.

Employees showed hard work, dedication and determination, and made meaningful gains.

PROFILE

The winning ways of Joe Cavanaugh

W hen Joe Cavanaugh took over the reins of **Local 270** (City of Spokane) in 1984 he faced challenges that threatened the very existence of the local union and Council 2 itself.

In the wake of the resignation of the former local president alleged to have misused as much as $40,000 in union funds, members were angry and disillusioned, contact with the City had broken down, and attempts were being made to decertify the 714-member union, Council 2's largest local. (*See Page 25.*)

Cavanaugh, a survey engineer with the City, slowly but steadily won back members' confidence with the honest, open, calm and unassuming manner that comes naturally to him.

"I met with the members and talked with them," he says. "I held innumerable meetings to try to explain what had happened and what we were doing in an attempt to recover the membership's trust. I confronted the allegations head-on."

At the same time, he ensured Local 270 was well run — financially and procedurally.

He met, too, with the City of Spokane, explaining what the local was doing and would do.

At times it seemed touch-and-go

JOE CAVANAUGH
LOCAL 270 PRESIDENT
1984–PRESENT

but, Cavanaugh says, he was given strong support by then Staff Representative John Cole and former Local 270 President Dean Berry. They formed a team that not only rescued the local, but strengthened it, too.

In the 30 years since then, Cavanaugh has led the local, which now numbers 1,050, with the same open communication, understanding and trust. "I have always believed we need to talk with the people we represent," he says. "I try to understand where members are coming from and what they want. Talking with them and listening to them is the best tonic."

2001

Workers rush to join Council 2

The number of unaffiliated workers seeking to join Council 2 has jumped sharply in the wake of voter approval of Initiative 747.

Approved in the November 2001 election, the initiative limits increases in property taxes to 1 percent a year without special voter approval.

Workers are concerned about job security and about wages and benefits, particularly medical benefits, being cut in the wake of the initiative.

The initiative is expected to have a strong impact on the income of counties and cities, particularly as the limit is less than the rate of inflation, now running at around 3 percent.

Many of the public agencies are looking at layoffs and budget cuts.

Suddenly, workers are seeing the benefits of belonging to a union.

Shelton bargained nearly 200 contracts

Kathleen Shelton bargained 150 to 200 contracts and handled 10 times as many grievances during her 21 years with Council 2. She served as education director and conducted steward training across the state.

Shelton joined Thurston County as a real estate appraiser in 1978 and soon worked her way up to president of **Local 618**.

In 1981 she joined Council 2 as a staff representative for all southwestern Washington locals, representing 1,000 to 1,200 members. "I think Council 2 does a fantastic job of representing people," Shelton said. "They have a professional staff and excellent leadership."

Shelton retired in February, 2002.

Proved to be excellent choice

T. Kae Roan served as Council 2 staff representative in the Pasco office for 12 years.

"Kae was the first person I hired after becoming president," says Council 2 President and Executive Director Chris Dugovich.

"She certainly proved to be a good choice. She did an excellent job."

Roan retired in August, 2002.

PROFILE

Ron Fredin's a true man of labor

He was born a labor guy. He speaks like a labor guy. And he fights for labor guys.

Meet Ron Fredin, Council 2 vice president and the quintessential — you guessed it — labor guy.

Not for him the fancy words that disguise what you're really saying and thinking. Down-to-earth and honest, he uses whatever language it takes to get his point across. As he puts it, "Sometimes you've got to speak the way of labor."

In 2003, Roy Brannam, left, handed over the vice-presidency reins to Ron Fredin, center. Congratulating them is Council 2 President/Executive Director Chris Dugovich.

RON FREDIN
VICE PRESIDENT 2003–PRESENT

Fredin joined the Streets Department at the City of Vancouver in 1981. He's been there ever since.

He soon became involved in Local 307-VC, alternating over the years between being president and vice-president of the local and leading about six major contract negotiations.

After being elected vice-president of Council 2 in 2003 he had to run his first meeting as chair of the legislative committee. In the room was Roy Brannam, the previous vice president.

"I was about as nervous as I could be," he recalls. "I realized I was filling the shoes of a legend. I involved him in that first meeting as a show of respect." And a way to calm his nerves.

His next big challenge was to open the biennial convention. Afterward, members came up to him and said, "You're going to be good. You're one of us." That was key. "I realized I had been brought into this world to fight for the labor guy and I cannot stop doing it," Fredin says. "It's in my blood."

2002

How Council 2 achieved its biggest organizing gain ever

All the effort put into a year-long campaign was rewarded December 3, 2002.

In an 88 percent turnout, librarians, library assistants and technicians in the King County Library voted 298 to 157 to join Council 2.

The gain of 550 new members is the largest local government election in memory Council 2 has won.

Council 2 President/Executive Director Chris Dugovich thanked full-time campaign assistant Susan Cole and Council 2 staff organizers Bill Keenan and Bill Dennis for their work in coordinating the campaign.

Keenan, who spearheaded the campaign, attributed the successful outcome to several factors.

• The organizing committee, who put huge amounts of their own time into the campaign.

• The leasing of a van to serve as a "vehicle for change." Dubbed the "KCLS (for King County Library

King County Library employees celebrate their decision to join Council 2.

Make a Choice
Gain a Voice
Union!

System) Organizing Van," it was driven to all 42 branches where organizing committee members helped distribute union materials and field questions.

• The hiring of Cole to work full-time on the campaign. A former president of the Pierce County Library Local, she is familiar with Council 2 as well as libraries.

Keenan says the library staff voted to join Council 2 because they believe the union can help them obtain a voice in the policies and procedures of the library and a say over their working conditions.

2003

Pension reform is approved

Pat Thompson, left, at signing of pensions bill.

Years of work by Council 2 on pension reform finally paid off this session. A measure signed into law on May 14 by Gov. Gary Locke, establishes a new pensions board on which the views of active and retired employees will be heard more strongly than with the previous board.

The new 20-member Joint Committee on Pension Policy (JCPP) will include four members representing active employees and two members representing retired employees.

Council 2 took the lead in working to achieve this breakthrough in pension governance. Pat Thompson, Council 2's Director of Legislation/Political Action, led a coalition of labor unions supporting the bill and testified before the committee.

Later in the year, Thompson was appointed by Gov. Locke to serve on the new committee.

2004

Pension body proves its worth

IN ONLY ITS FIRST YEAR, the new 20-member Joint Committee on Pension Policy (*see above*) has been instrumental in the passing of three bills that will improve Council 2 members' pension benefits.

Job retention becomes the major issue

A decade ago, workers were fighting for higher wages to keep pace with inflation. About three years ago, they were more concerned about benefits, and particularly health benefits.

Now the pendulum has swung again and workers are placing a higher priority, above all, on retaining their jobs. The new mood reflects the changing economic climate and particularly budget cuts, which have reduced the rolls of county and city employees.

Workers see Council 2 as a major force in helping them to retain their positions.

PROFILE

Don Boxford's career spanned 30 years

DON BOXFORD
STAFF REP.
1993–2013

K nown as "Box," Don Boxford always had a great way of telling a story in his trademark Oklahoma accent.

He also had an inner patience that survived any situation.

These two personality traits made Boxford a difficult guy for the employer to say "no" to.

After leaving Weyerhaeuser in the wake of cutbacks in the lumber industry, Boxford went to work for Snohomish County as a diesel mechanic in 1979. He became active in **Local 109**, serving as a shop steward, vice-president and more than 10 years as president.

Among his accomplishments were the first employer-paid full-family medical plan and the first master agreement covering all Snohomish County local unions (*see Page 62*). As part of that settlement, he was instrumental in a Superior Court Award that retained the Step Plan and was worth more than $1.2 million to members.

In 1993 he became a staff representative, taking care of Council 2's locals in Central Washington.

After hundreds of contracts and many miles on the road, Boxford retired in 2013.

Non-profit gain is a first

For the first time, employees at a private non-profit company have joined Council 2. Twenty-one residential support staff at **Twin Harbors Group Home** in Aberdeen became members of the union after a Jan. 14, 2004 vote.

Popular weekend event returns

THE COUNCIL 2 PRESIDENTS CONFERENCE is back. It's all new and better than before.

To be held October 29–30, 2004 in the Wenatchee Convention Center, it is open to the presidents of all Council 2 local unions. Topics to be covered will be collective bargaining, political races and legal trends. *The conference has been held every year since then.*

2005

Master contract covers 4 locals

After more than a year's intensive bargaining, a Snohomish County Master Agreement covering some 1,300 workers was ratified in September. The agreement applies from this year through 2008.

Covering several local unions at the same time, master agreements set out basic principles that apply to all the locals involved. Each bargaining unit negotiates its own addendum that outlines specific issues that relate only to that work group.

The Snohomish County Master Agreement covers **Locals 109, 109-E, 1811-C** and **1811-CA**.

In addition Superior Court employees represented by 1811-JPD and District Court employees in 1811-CA also ratified economic and non-economic agreements for the same period as the Master Agreement.

"We achieved many of our goals," says James Trefry, the Council 2 staff representative who led the negotiations.

"The contract gives our members a larger percentage of the cost-of-living adjustments than any previous contract."

Medical contributions are locked in at the 2004 level.

Appeal is first of its sort

When an arbitrator ruled in favor of Council 2 earlier this year, Benton County took the unusual step of appealing the ruling to the Superior Court. The county contested the decision by Arbitrator Michael Cavanaugh that a terminated court recorder should be reinstated to her position with full pay

and benefits.

"In at least the last 14 years at Council 2, such an appeal has never been lodged before," says Dave Kanigel, who represented the union in both hearings.

But the county also lost the appeal. Judge William Acey from nearby Asotin County ordered the county to comply with the arbitrator's decision.

THE PERCENTAGE of full dues paying members in Idaho has grown to nearly 75 percent from less than 40 percent 15 years ago. The figure is impressive; union membership in Idaho, a right to work state, is voluntary.

2005

Spokane County employees receive big payout

About 862 current and former Spokane County employees will receive checks totaling $227,805 following the settlement of a lawsuit between Council 2 and Spokane County. Amounts paid to each member range from $3,600 to less than a dollar.

Council 2 argued a portion of a payment by Standard Insurance Company to Spokane County should have been passed on to employees, but was not.

AT THE GOLF TOURNAMENT held at the start of Council 2's biennial convention in Spokane in 2005, union members not only played the course, they were also involved in maintaining it.

The Creek at Qualchan is run by the City of Spokane and the grounds are maintained by members of **Local 270**.

Members who played the course undoubtedly admired the handiwork of their fellow union members as they sank those putts.

2006

Harry got the job done

Harry Laube — former long-time staff representative — seemed to have the perfect characteristics to handle being a union person.

He was someone you could count on to complete the job. He knew everyone and everyone knew him.

"He enjoyed it and nothing ever seemed to remotely bother him," says Council 2 President Chris Dugovich. "His patience and his good nature carried him through difficult assignments filled with difficult people.

"There was never more of a gentleman who was liked, enjoyed and respected by all."

After he was hired by the Bellingham Water Department in the early fifties Laube became increasingly active in **Local 114**. As local president he ushered in the new era of collective bargaining that began in 1967. He was hired by Council 2 as a staff representative in 1969.

Laube retired in 1979, but continued to work for Council 2 on a temporary basis into the nineties.

2007

Pension gain:

Best in 20 years

The most significant improvement in local government employees' pensions in at least 20 years has been signed into law by Gov. Christine Gregoire.

The new law will benefit all Public Employees Retirement System participants. But the benefit that will affect Council 2 members most is the lowering of career employees' retirement age from 65 to 62.

Council 2's Deputy Director Pat Thompson, who took a lead in having the legislation passed, worked on it for years.

Since 1977, most Council 2 members have been required to work until age 65 regardless of their years of service. The penalty for retiring earlier was lessened in 2000, when it was lowered to 3 percent for every year employees left before age 65 (*See page 54*).

Now the new law provides no penalty for retiring at 62 or later with 30

> # The new law provides no penalty for retiring at 62 or later with 30 years of service.

years of service.

"These new provisions are a significant improvement for career employees and will provide a realistic option for our members who find themselves working in jobs that are not conducive to working to age 65," Thompson said.

KATHLEEN ETHEREDGE of Local 2617 (City of Kent) has been elected Council 2's secretary-treasurer. She replaces Judy Johnson, who retired after serving in the position for 16 years. (*See Page 34*)

Etheredge comes to the position with strong qualifications as she is a senior financial analyst with the City of Kent.

She intends to follow in Johnson's footsteps. "I have big shoes to fill," she says.

PROFILE

How Pat Thompson made his mark on Olympia

When it comes to recent pension improvements, Deputy Director Pat Thompson is the man Council 2 members need to thank.

He has worked tirelessly over two decades with state legislators in Olympia to secure a better pension deal for Council 2 members. It has not been easy. Not only did he navigate the complex and often arcane field of pension policy with the skill of a master, he also secured the gains at a time when the legislature was trying to reduce, not improve, benefits.

Thompson helped form the Joint Committee on Pension Policy, on which he serves, which put labor in the front seats of pension policy (*see Page 60*). And he played a major role in having the normal retirement age cut from 65 to 62 without penalty for those with 30 years service (*see Page 64*).

Thompson built on expertise he first learned in 1989 from Sam Kinville, who was then a Council 2 lobbyist and whom he met almost by accident at a Council 2 convention.

"We struck up a relationship," Thompson recalls. "He suggested I get involved in political action for the union. He took me under his wing."

He could not have hoped for a more knowledgeable tutor than Kinville, who understood better than

PAT THOMPSON
DEPUTY DIRECTOR
1994–PRESENT

most how politics worked in Olympia.

When Kinville left Council 2 in 1994, Thompson was appointed Director of Legislation/Political Action, a duty he still performs in addition to that of Deputy Director.

He has proven a worthy successor to Kinville. In addition to his work on pensions, among his achievements in Olympia was ensuring that bargaining rights were restored to deputy prosecutors after they had been taken away eight years before by the Supreme Court (*see Page 54*).

Another highlight: campaigning for Sen. Maria Cantwell in 2002, whose win has been positive for the union, he says.

2008

The day the pages turned

It took a lot of campaigning over several months in rough weather, but the result was worth it. About 400 pages at the King County Library System have joined Council 2 as a result.

The addition of the pages means almost all non-management workers in the library system have joined Council 2. (*See Page 59.*)

Council 2 Director of Organizing Bill Keenan looks on as Susan Allen and Karen Russell mail authorization cards for the King County Library System pages election.

The movement to unionize began in December 2006.

Pages had seen the benefits enjoyed by the other 550 library workers after they joined the union nearly six years ago. They had many issues they felt needed to be addressed. They wanted in, too.

Council 2 staff sprung into action.

"We formed an organizing committee and began campaigning for members to sign authorization cards," says Council 2 Director of Organizing Bill Keenan.

Because the union could not campaign inside the libraries, the organizing committee set up tables in the parking lots outside the branches. They published two flyers over several months to help get the message across.

"They had to try to reach as many of the 42 branches as they could. They also had to work during one of the harshest winters the Pacific Northwest has experienced in recent memory."

The election result: 142-58 in favor of joining Council 2, a margin of about two-to-one.

On July 7, the pages were certified as an official bargaining unit represented by Council 2.

Keenan praises Susan Allen, a page at the Bellevue library, the largest branch in the King County Library System, for the effort she put into signing up her fellow pages and in coordinating the campaign.

PROFILE

Few can match Bill Keenan's organizing skills

BILL KEENAN
ORGANIZING
DIRECTOR
1998-PRESENT

When 400 library pages joined Council 2 in 2008 (*see Page 66*), Bill Keenan was elated. With the previous win of some 500 library workers (*see Page 59*), it was a highlight in his career as a union organizer.

Since he joined Council 2 as a staff representative in Spokane in 1984, Council 2 has gained close to 10,000 new members. That's an average 330 a year — a number that few organizers in any union can match.

It's a job he relishes. "Being a union organizer is the greatest opportunity of any position to meet and work with hundreds of people over the years," he says.

Keenan joined the Service Employees International Union (SEIU) in the late 70s while working for the City of Coeur d'Alene.

In 1982, after helping organize the city workers, he worked full-time for SEIU for two years before becoming Council 2's first full-time staff representative in Spokane.

In 1998 he was named Organizing Director for Council 2 and moved to the Everett headquarters.

Not only has he gained many new members for the union over the years, he also has served as an adviser in many negotiations and assisted in strikes.

Main reason workers join unions

The reasons workers join a union, no matter where and when, are dignity and respect. Nothing else. That is Bill Keenan's conclusion after gaining thousands of new members for Council 2 over 30 years.

"I have never run into workers wanting to join a union because they were underpaid," Keenan says. "Working conditions, however, affect your health, your family and your quality of life. People will leave the highest-paid positions if they are treated poorly."

2008

Budget crisis hits
'We're working to lessen the impact'

These are difficult times for local governments across the state when it comes to budgeting.

Income from taxes and other sources has plummeted, making it difficult for local governments to balance their books without cutting back on staff.

"In my close to 27 years, I've never seen the type of job losses that are likely to occur in 2009," says Council 2 President/Executive Director Chris Dugovich. "In Snohomish County alone, where construction has ground to a stop, more than 150 of our members may face a new year looking for new employment.

"Council 2 is doing its best to attempt to lessen the blow to as many members as possible. We will emphasize that cuts need to be across the board, affecting management as well as rank and file.

"We can be thankful that our local industry is not falling apart like the auto companies in the Midwest. We will come out of this, and in the meantime we will be working to save as many local government positions as possible."

2009

Library staff take week's furlough

Faced with budget shortfalls and the prospect of layoffs, some Council 2 locals have agreed to take a day's furlough here and there during the year. But **Local 2083**, representing staff at the Seattle Public Library, agreed to take a full week of unpaid leave all at once: From August 31 to September 8, 2009.

The reason: The budget crisis facing the library is more severe than in other cases and needed drastic action more quickly. And the loss of a week's pay was preferable to layoffs.

"The staff at the Seattle Public Library is fully aware of the economic hardship our country and community is going through," said Local 2083 President Dave Lonergan. "We see it every day as we help our patrons."

The staff used the time off to provide community service.

Support for Local 2083 came from Seattle Mayor Greg Nickels.

"What is heartwarming to me is that they decided to take the week off without pay rather than see their fellow workers lose their jobs."

2010

Furloughs threaten to turn into cutbacks and layoffs

The impact of the worst recession since the 1930s is hitting home in cities and counties across the state.

Faced with sharply lower income, local governments are being forced to cut their budgets for this year and next more severely than they had at first thought would be necessary.

Cutting budgets means cutting costs and often those costs are services provided by Council 2 members.

As a result, last year's furloughs are turning into the threat of more severe cutbacks and layoffs this year in the face of sharply lower cash flows.

As the pressure mounts, Council 2 staffers are seeking to find solutions, to become creative and to bargain aggressively to counter the impact on members as much as possible.

Because layoffs or furloughs are mandatory subjects of bargaining under state law, Council 2 can raise those issues at the bargaining table, proposing cutbacks elsewhere, such as in materials or benefits, rather than cuts in staffing or payrolls.

Council 2 staffers are holding ongoing discussions with local government administrators, using their years of expertise in negotiating to do all they can to mitigate the effects of the budget shortfalls on members.

An area strongly hit is residential construction, which has fallen faster than anticipated. The slump — a result of the housing crash — leads to fewer building permits, lower income from real estate excise taxes as fewer houses are sold, and lower property taxes as values drop.

An example of the situation being experienced across Washington is the City of Seattle where Mayor Mike McGinn has asked all departments to suggest reductions of 3 percent for their 2010 mid-term budgets.

The recession led to a loss of 14,600 jobs in the Seattle metro area and 119,000 in Puget Sound.

It also led to a collapse in the housing market and a 33.3 percent fall in construction.

As a result, the tax base from which the city derives its income suffered its biggest decline since at least 1974.

"Looking back, I think what stands out right now is how difficult doing this job has become with the current state of the economy." — *Staff Representative Dennis Bolton, on his retirement in 2011.*

2010

Persist, persist and persist again...and you will succeed

Talk about persistence. It would take a lot to beat that shown by **Local 120** President John Ohlson, whose persistance lasted for eight years.

The tale of tenacity starts in 2002:

▶ Ohlson points out to the City of Tacoma that 26 business analysts are doing union-covered work,

John Ohlson

but they don't have the benefit of being union members.

▶ No, says the city. In 18 months the group will be reassigned to uncovered positions when their project is complete. It makes no sense to have them join the union and then leave it.

▶ Not good enough, says Ohlson. Once the project is complete, they will continue to do union work, although their job descriptions might change.

▶ No, says the City, applying a generic description of "management analyst" to the employees to keep them from being classified as union workers.

▶ Not good enough, says

Ohlson. The City should follow a ruling by the Joint Labor Committee that the new positions will be union jobs as long as the employees are doing union-covered work.

▶ No, says the City. They won't classify them as union workers.

▶ Ohlson launches an organizing drive to prepare for an election in which the workers will vote for or against being part of Local 120.

▶ Some discontented workers leave. Ohlson has to start the drive over again with the new employees.

▶ The City challenges the validity of the voting and reclassifies the 26 workers as "business analysts."

▶ In 2010 Ohlson decides to "roll the dice." He calls an election.

The result: 14 votes in favor of joining Council 2, seven against and five abstentions.

▶ The analysts join the other 700 Local 120 members on April 27 when the election is certified.

Ohlson retired in 2012.

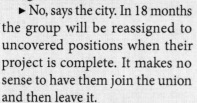

2011

Attack on unions is unnerving

Council 2 is worried the attack on public employee unions, seen as the most intensive in at least 30 years, might spread to Washington state.

Although the state remains generally pro-union, the removal of bargaining rights in Wisconsin, where AFSCME was born, is unnerving members here.

Right-to-work legislation is being introduced in more and more states, but the major attack is on collective bargaining. In at least eight states workers' right to collectively bargain has been encroached upon.

Convention is golden

COUNCIL 2's convention — held at the Westin Hotel, Seattle, in June, 2011 — was its 50th.

At the biennial conventions, members express their views on the direction the union should take through resolutions and constitutional amendments as well as the election of office bearers. Workshops are also held. (*See Page 71.*)

2013

Improving economy brings relief to employees

City and county employees are starting to climb out of the deep hole into which the 2007–2009 Great Recession plunged them.

Wages are increasing, layoffs have decreased, and some jurisdictions are even hiring new workers.

"Some employers have settled multiple-year agreements, with increases averaging around 2 percent," says Council 2 Director of Organizing Bill Keenan. "Although we are a long way from a full recovery, the situation is in strong contrast to that four years ago when we were looking at wage givebacks, wage freezes, furloughs and significant layoffs."

The public sector tends to lag the general economy, he adds. Just as it took a while before the full force of the recession hit the public sector, so the public sector is now following the uptick in the general economy that began a couple of years ago.

2014

$1.3-million settlement is largest ever for Council 2 members

Snohomish County members will enjoy lower payroll deductions for health insurance from July until April 2015 — and possibly for longer — thanks to a settlement between the county and Council 2.

The county will transfer $1.3 million into the union's health insurance fund to cover the payroll deductions.

The new lower rates are locked in until April next year and lower premiums will continue until the money runs out.

The settlement, the largest ever received by Council 2 members, was a result of a complaint filed in August 2013 by the union against Snohomish County for underfunding its plan at a time of multiple layoffs and wage freezes.

"To their credit, the administration officials were willing to work with us," Council 2 President/Executive Officer Chris Dugovich said.

State Supreme Court Decision:

PERS 2 'Early Retirement Factors' survive

In a much anticipated ruling, the State Supreme Court has over-turned the lower court's opinion and upheld a law passed in 2007 which repealed "gain sharing" and lowered the normal retirement age from 65 to 62 for members with 30 years of service. (*See Page 64*)

Council 2 was a major supporter of the measure.

The passage of this bill and the subsequent Supreme Court ruling preserves the largest improvement in Plan 2 since its inception.

Many members had been await-ing this ruling because if the court upheld gain sharing, the Early Retirement Factors could have been eliminated.

"It's finally over and the 'legal certainty' required to maintain the benefits we gained has been reached," says Council 2 Deputy Director Pat Thompson.

CONVENTIONS

The biennial convention, held in venues around the state, has always been one of the most important events on the Council 2 calendar. Here's why:

• The convention provides delegates with the opportunity to participate in the running of the union, particularly through the resolutions adopted at the plenary session and the election of office bearers.

• Workshops impart valuable information on key aspects of union activity.

• Labor and political leaders deliver speeches that encourage and inspire members.

• Union dedication is recognized in congratulatory speeches and the annual Hersey Awards.

• Delegates interact with others, both socially and in union business.

• The convention also provides opportunities for relaxation and fellowship. From the Friday golf tournament to the Saturday dinner-dance and the evening hospitality rooms, delegates have fun between the times of hard work and learning. And it all adds to the spirit of friendship and togetherness.

Convention life is reflected in pictures on this page and the next.

Convention in session in Spokane in 2009.

MANY COUNCIL 2 members find lifelong friends through the union, particularly when sharing in activities, such as those at conventions, conferences and the annual Legislative Weekend.

The Women's Action Committee, for example, has bonded over the years. A retiring member said she would miss her fellow committee members more than her job and her fellow employees. "You are like sisters to me," she said at a 2005 convention breakfast. Another retiree said she would miss them "even more than my dog or cat."

Valerie Davis of Local 1811CA addresses the 1993 convention.

Spokane County delegates applaud a speaker at the 1997 convention.

Left: Host committee dressed up for the dinner-dance at the 2009 convention in Spokane.

Below: Swearing in the new executive board, 2005.

Workshop at the 2005 convention.

Decades of dedication

Giving a lifetime of service

In many industries today, workers devote only a few years to a company before they move on to another position in another firm, often for more pay or better working conditions. The result is that new employees have to be trained and gather experience at the company's expense before becoming an asset to the organization.

Public service employees who are members of a union like Council 2, however, tend to devote many years of service to their careers. Over time, they become more and more proficient and find ways to perform their jobs even better.

The reason is that, as members of Council 2, they can be assured of decent wages, good working conditions, job security and solid medical and pension benefits. So they stay where they are, often for decades.

The benefits to cities and counties are immense.

In the coming pages we highlight a few of the many Council 2 members who not only have given the best years of their lives to public service, but have devoted many years to Council 2, knowing that the union is key to making their careers more rewarding.

2005

30+ YEARS

Library staff honored

Forty-four Seattle Public Library staff members — many members of Council 2's **Local 2083** —were honored January 26, 2005 for more than 30 years service to the library.

The awards were presented at a special Service Awards Ceremony held by the board of trustees.

See below for a profile of one such long-serving library staffer.

Staffer merged hobby and work

Working in the auto repair collection at the Seattle Public Library is more than a daytime job for Eric Cisney. It fits right in with his love for repairing broken-down vehicles and restoring vintage cars.

39 YEARS He has devoted almost 39 years of his working life at the library to develop and update an index to the auto manuals to help mechanics from across the state find what they need.

Back home, he's at his happiest tinkering with automobiles.

On the 15 acres of land he owns in Port Orchard are vehicles ranging from a World War II Dodge ambulance, a 1957 Chevrolet pick-up truck or a VW Beetle.

Eric Cisney

Cisney helped establish **Local 2083** at the library. He served as union president for six years, helping to negotiate three labor contracts.

Cisney retired from public service in 2006.

2006

Nothing stood in her way

Margaret Ziegler

Almost from the day Margaret Ziegler began work at the Bellingham Public Library in July 1970, she set a priority on being involved in a union. But she had to start from scratch because the library workers were not organized.

It was unusual in those days for librarians to join unions. They were considered exempt employees. But Ziegler was not one to let such obstacles stand in her way. By 1974 the librarians, (**34 YEARS**) led by Ziegler, had become members of Council 2. And, again at Ziegler's insistence, they soon had their own local — **114-L.**

During her 34 years at the library, Ziegler set a record by being Local president for more than 25 years of the Local's 31-year existence.

Ziegler says librarians are interested in public service, highly motivated and educated, and care about the community.

"They also care about being treated fairly when it comes to wages and working conditions.

Tips for success

• Don't make assumptions about anything; always get it in writing.
• Date everything.
• Be prepared for meetings — anticipate management's positions and discuss them with your Staff Representative.
• Ask questions. Don't be afraid to express strong opinions and to challenge management's positions.
• Communication is key. Be open on the issues.

— Margaret Ziegler

"That's where the union comes in because it is a professional organization and has provided us with professional help at the bargaining table and important support in grievance matters."

Ziegler retired at the end of 2005 as head of reference services.

2006

Council 2 brought big gains, says oldest living member

When members of **Local 1135** in Spokane County recently celebrated their 50th anniversary since becoming organized, they presented a plaque to Glenn Spear, 81, who is the only living charter member.

Among a handful of shop workers who first organized the road department employees, Spear says the main reasons they organized were their working conditions — six-day work weeks, no overtime pay, no sick leave and being at-will employees.

Those conditions improved dramatically after they joined Council 2.

Glenn Spear holds a plaque presented to him by local members.

Planner promoted trails and charitable causes

Ron Alldredge

RON ALLDREDGE, who died March 22, 2006 after a 10-month battle with liver cancer, began work as an associate planner in the Snohomish County Planning and Development Services Department (**Local 109-E**) in 1976.

(**29 YEARS**)

A senior planner for most of his 29-year career, he served on the board of Community Transit and the Snohomish City Council from 1978 to 1989, serving twice as Mayor Pro-Tem. A devoted advocate of community trails, he shepherded the vision for the Snohomish Riverfront Trail through public review. He died shortly before the trail was formally opened. He also promoted a variety of charitable causes.

"His co-workers loved and respected him for his kindness, integrity, knowledge and sheer spunk," says Vel Smith, human resources coordinator for Planning and Development Services.

"He was passionate about civic service. Everything he did, he did with his whole heart. We miss him."

2008

Bus driver makes her final stop after three decades

For Gloria Day, retiring is bitter-sweet. After 32 years on the job, she says she will have a hard time giving up her position as a bus driver for the Aberdeen School District as well as her work for Council 2 as a union member and officer of **Local 275** in Grays Harbor. Both the job and the union have been her passion.

"I knew from the start it was a job I would retire from,"

32 YEARS

she says. "I loved the kids and every part of it. And I loved being a union representative. It is so rewarding making the jobs of your fellow workers a little easier. There is not a better union than Council 2."

The children she drove when they were toting lunch boxes still remember her now that they are putting their own kids on the bus.

And she occupies an exceptional

Aberdeen School bus driver Gloria Day, of Local 275, ensures special needs student Rosaliea Holman is safely buckled in for her ride home.

place in the hearts of the special needs children she has been driving for the last five years.

WHEN JOANNE VAUGHN became secretary treasurer of **Local 270** (City of Spokane), she succeeded in the challenging task of restoring the books to a professional level. At that time she joined the

25 YEARS

Women's Action Committee and remained a member until her retirement in 2005. She was one of only two women in the Solid Waste Department office and was shop steward in the Refuse Department when no one else would undertake the task.

2009

Library worker brought out sun on cloudy days

When Norma Kremser began her career at Whatcom County Library System in 1976, she worked in a middle school training students in each home room to run a 16mm film projector. Over the years, Norma kept pace with the changes, working with video and DVD, CD-ROM and now even MP3 and downloadable formats.

33 YEARS

Norma Kremser

She wore many hats during her years of service to the Whatcom County Library System, but she will also be remembered for her green thumb and fingers that are nimble with a needle, said Lisa Gresham, **Local 1581.**

"Her quilt works adorning our building have turned many cloudy northwest days into sunny ones.

"We thank Norma for her 33 years of dedicated service."

'Without the union you have nothing'

Doug Peterson

Council 2 members likely know Doug Peterson best as the sergeant-at-arms at numerous conventions over the years. But not only was he an active member of **Local 21**, but he also served for many years on the Council 2 executive board, representing District Two.

26 YEARS

Now he has hung up his union hat after retiring from his 26-year career as a truck driver with the City of Seattle.

"Being a member of the union is extremely important," he says. "I would advise young people to listen to the oldies and to become involved in the union; without it you have nothing."

2010

Making life better for others

When next you wait at a light before crossing the road, glance down at the dip in the sidewalk that allows those in wheelchairs to use the crossing. Then give a thought for those who built the facility — people like Jack Aubrey, Seattle City worker and **Local 21** president.

Jack Aubrey

(**30 YEARS**) "Our satisfaction is that we are giving people accessibility to cross the street," says Aubrey. "We're giving them a facility so they don't have to bounce their wheelchairs up or down the curb, which could cause them to lose their balance or topple."

Creating ramps is only part of what Aubrey, a truck driver who lives in Shoreline, does these days in his work for the City of Seattle. The major part of his work is repairing main arterials and residential streets. His 30 years of public service and the experience he has gained over that time smooth the way for others to live just that little bit better.

He set high work standards

Chuck Thompson, 66, who died in a car accident in early April 2010, loved his work as a radio technician for the City of Seattle's Transportation Department.

"It was not just a job," says long-time co-worker Molly Lawless, a fellow member of **Local 21**. "He was extremely professional. He would welcome being called out at 2 a.m. He was so good two people will have to replace him."

Thompson — who was responsible for maintaining all the two-way radios in the department's 500 vehicles, as well as four transmitting towers — was a dedicated union member who contributed insight at meetings, Transportation Director

Chuck Thompson
(Photo: Suzie Weida)

Peter Hahn said. "A dedicated professional, he performed his duties with great care and pride."

2012

It's a TOUGH job —
but there are BRIGHT spots

Corrections officer Tom Trarbough performs a tough job, one most people do not want to even hear about, let alone do.

It's unpleasant, it's challenging and it can be soul-destroying.

"We have had several people who have tried the job but they have not been able to do it," says Trarbough, who is a sergeant at the Spokane County Jail,

Tom Trarbough

27 YEARS

president of **Local 492-CS** and a member of Council 2's Executive Board.

"Society wants people locked up, but as long as they are off the streets they don't give them — or corrections officers — much thought. Yet we are dealing with the worst of society."

And it's not getting any better. "The inmates — who are increasing in number — are more aggressive and more violent than they were just a few years ago," Trarbough says. "They could care less about authority and are younger when they end up here.

"The situation is compounded by those who carry disease or who have mental-health issues. We're like a second mental-health facility because the states have cut back so much on their spending on mental-health facilities.

But there are bright spots. One is being a member of a union. When young people come into the workforce, they often criticize unions, says Trarbough, a member of Council 2 for the 27 years he has worked as a Spokane County corrections officer. "But they don't realize how far unions have brought us and how much we still need them," he says.

"I think Council 2 does a phenomenal job in the way they help us negotiate better wage and medical packages. I came from a job that didn't have a union and the wages reflected that. It is great to have a union that can protect your interests in the workplace and ensure you have a good retirement plan."

2012

He turned his job into a calling

Two aspects of his working life set Joe Frisino apart.

• The first is that he retired from the King County Medical Examiner's Office, where he was a member of **Local 1652,** after doing the same job there for an amazing 44 years.

Joe Frisino

• The second is that he turned what could have been a routine job into a dedication to honoring our society's lost, forgotten and discarded.

Frisino began work as an investigator in 1968 at what was then known as the King County Coroner's office. When he was summoned to a death scene, he was part of a team mandated to determine the cause of death and determine the person's identity.

44 YEARS

But, as he worked his way up to lead investigator and visited more and more death scenes, Frisino became concerned about the people who died alone.

Did family, close friends and associates. even know of this person's death?

If they did, how would they cope?

Frisino dedicated more of his time to finding out who they were and tracing their families or friends.

When Frisino and his fellow workers were able to trace some relatives, they often found that those people were unable to help with the burial.

Frisino stepped in and worked with religious leaders of every denomination to provide them with funeral services.

They were buried in a cement vault in the Renton area about every 18 months.

"I saw a need there," he says. "These people needed a burial with dignity."

In addition, Frisino was concerned about the suicides that were part of his investigation.

He helped set up the Survivors of Suicide Group (SOS) in the early 1990s that works not only with those contemplating suicide but also helps the families, significant others and friends to cope.

Frisino says Council 2 enabled him and his fellow workers to gain good contracts and so enabled him to devote his life to his work.

2012

Helping troubled young people has its own reward

The reward for being a juvenile counselor, Michael West says, comes when the young people you have helped return and say "thank you."

"You feel your interaction with them served a purpose.

"I would like to think that I have helped out and made a difference in the lives of young people and their families."

That is clearly an understatement; West touched hundreds of young people's lives over many years, helping them cope and steering them away from a life of crime.

(**25 YEARS**)

After studying at the University of Nebraska in Omaha, West worked as a drug and alcohol counselor with Eastern Nebraska Human Services.

He moved to Seattle in 1979 where he worked for Pioneer Human Services, a then nationally recognized program for providing drug and alcohol services.

In 1987 he began working for King County, first as a juvenile detention officer and later as a detention officer, drug and alcohol outreach specialist, gang offender specialist and probation counselor, a position he held from 1996 until he retired in 2012.

Michael West

"Out of all the positions, I think I enjoyed the gang unit the most; it was more challenging, not just in the gang aspect, but being involved in different aspects of the justice system."

West served as president of **Local 2084-SC** and also was a member of the local's executive board.

Over this time, West says, he has learned how important union membership is, "especially in these times when a lot of workers are viewed as being a problem rather than a model for decent wages and working conditions," he adds.

Going beyond the call

Quality shines through

I t's true that public employees who are union members take pride in what they do. After all, as dedicated, hard workers, they take their role of serving the public seriously.

But at times they go beyond the call of duty.

For that, they are recognized by those they serve as special people.

In the following pages, we recall occasions when members and staff have been honored, whether it be for longevity of service, outstanding volunteer work, an exceptional act of bravery, or simply excelling at what they do.

It's all part of quality people doing extra-quality work.

1982

Local president to serve on national committee

Merrie Sullivan, President of **Local 120-SCH**, has been appointed by International President Gerald McEntee to serve on the International Union School Employees Advisory Committee.

She attended a meeting in Washington, D.C. to consider such issues as the status of federal programs in public schools and efforts to fight cutbacks in services and layoffs of workers.

Mrs. Sullivan reported that much of the problems facing public school employees today is due to the "horrendous Republican policies" advocated by President

Merrie Sullivan

'Only 8 percent of the budget is for educational programs'

Reagan and noted that only 8 percent of the budget is for educational programs.

Another serious issue is the increasing practice of contracting out school services. In addition to costing AFSCME members their jobs, contracting out also results in the reduction of quality of services. The committee saw evidence of firms which hire into schools with low bids, work well for a while, and then raise prices out of bounds for the sake of profit.

Council 2 President Larry McKibben praised Mrs. Sullivan for her excellent work on the committee and thanked her for her efforts against the contracting out of food services in the schools.

"I consider this to be one of the lowest tricks in the world," he said. "To take food from the mouths of children for the sake of profit is ugly."

1992

Local 120 member named:

EMPLOYEE VOLUNTEER OF THE YEAR

Carol Kruckeberg

Carol Kruckeberg, a member of Local 120, has been named Tacoma Public Utilities' employee volunteer of the year.

The award, presented by the Public Utilities Department, recognizes employees who give their time and talents to the community.

Kruckeberg has been the moving force behind the Utilities Department's involvement in Paint Tacoma-Pierce County Beautiful for two years.

A City Light senior warehouse technician, she also has been active in a host of other projects, including the Titlow Beach cleanup, Battered Women's Shelter, wildlife education, Big Brothers, Big Sisters, church activities and United Way.

But she has not been content in doing only those volunteer activities.

She also has volunteered for mountain rescue, senior citizen homes and Tacoma General Hospital geriatrics visiting, Tacoma General emergency room, and supporting the arts and the Snake Lake project.

It is indeed, an impressive list of achievements.

1995

Worker honored for helping save man's life

Dean Bachmeier.

Heavy equipment operator Dean Bachmeier has received a "Superior Service Award" from Spokane mayor Jack Geraghty, and the city council.

Bachmeier, a member of **Local 270**, was working at the Valley Transfer Station when he saw a person having a heart attack. He calmly instructed city workers to call 911 while he took charge of the situation, said Dennis Hein, director of the Spokane Solid Waste Management Department.

"Even after the paramedics had arrived, Mr. Bachmeier continued to administer CPR at the Fire Department's request," Hein added. "I believe the actions exhibited by Mr. Bachmeier exemplify superior service." Vance Lorive, the man who suffered the heart attack, is doing well, thanks to Bachmeier's prompt action.

1999

Wayne Parsley is a star among bus drivers across the nation.

Recently the member of **Local 1122** in Yakima won first place in the 35-foot bus category at the International Bus Roadeo competition in New York City.

Parsley guided a 35-foot bus through 11 obstacle courses, scoring 610 out of 650 points in 6 minutes, 8 seconds. His closest competitor was a few car lengths behind him and scored only 579 points.

1999

Prompt action by Council 2 members prevents catastrophe

When a pipeline exploded in Bellingham in late 1999, City employees (**Local 114**) kept the explosion—as bad as it was—from turning into a city-wide catastrophe.

The drama began when Don Alderson, a Water Department employee, called in to report an outdoor odor. Whatever the smell was, he told dispatchers, it was coming from Whatcom Creek, near his house. Fire Department dispatcher Cindy Sleuys issued an evacuation alert to fire fighters who had by now arrived at the creek.

But it was too late. Fumes from 277,000 gallons of gasoline that had leaked from the ruptured pipeline exploded in a fireball that burned more than a mile of park land.

The explosion claimed the lives of a teenage boy and two 10-year-old boys who, authorities said, set off the explosion by playing with a lighter.

Alderson was unhurt, but his home was destroyed.

Sleuys stayed at her post to direct emergency personnel. Two hours elapsed before she knew whether her husband, a fireman whom she had dispatched to the scene, was alive.

AFSCME members throughout the city rushed to respond to the emergency. The explosion nearly destroyed the city's wastewater treatment plant, which serves about 70,000 people. Restoring power to the plant was necessary to prevent a more widespread disaster from exposure to contaminated water.

"At one time, we were down to a foot-and-a-half, about an hour's supply, in one of the reservoirs," says Chuck Berlemann, a maintenance technician with the Public Works Department. Power finally was restored to the pumps and the water pressure was raised. A wider catastrophe had been averted.

> ## Council 2 members who helped
>
> These Council 2 members assisted in the 1999 Bellingham pipeline explosion: Dispatchers: Stephanie Haller, Faith Foster and Cindy Sleuys. Public Works Employees: Harvey Berwick, Jay Greenwood, Myron Hendrickson, Robyn Arbogast, Keith Smith, Myron Carlson, Kip Dunlap, Chuck Berlemann, Gary Gilfrilen and Ricky McWilliams.

2002

Officer saves woman as she takes 20-foot plunge

A heroic act by Spokane County Corrections Dept. Officer Tom Frantz probably saved a woman's life.

Frantz, a member of **Local 492**, caught the woman and broke her fall as she leaped from a railing in the corrections center.

Frantz, 39, was in a small interview cubicle at the base of the corrections building's mezzanine

Tom Frantz demonstrates how he broke an inmate's fall

stairs when a 22-year-old woman ran up the stairs and climbed on the railing. Frantz ran out of the cubicle and ordered the woman off the railing.

She ignored him and climbed higher, reaching 20 feet from the floor. Realizing he could not reach her in time by climbing the stairs, Frantz moved to where he calculated she would land should she jump. Within seconds, the woman, who weighs 135 pounds, dived backward, falling into Frantz's outstretched arms.

"I couldn't actually catch her, but I broke her fall," Frantz recalls.

The woman suffered a cracked pelvis and was hospitalized overnight.

Frantz suffered minor injuries, but he was back at work the next day.

Frantz credits his ability to act as he did to being a member of Local 492. "The union encouraged the administration to give me the training I received," Frantz said. "Without a strong union such as the one we belong to, a lot of the training sessions associated with taking action like this might not have been possible."

"Frantz's heroic act is an example of how his line of work is becoming increasingly dangerous due to the kind of prisoners that are being held in the corrections center," said Council 2 Staff Representative Gordon Smith.

"It makes their jobs all the more dangerous and challenging."

2005

Chosen as 'employee of the year' from 772 candidates

When the announce-ment was made that **Local 2617** president Kathleen Senecaut had been selected as Employee of the Year at the Kent Mayor's monthly breakfast meeting in February every employee stood. The applause was long and loud. She clearly was a popular choice.

Kathleen Senecaut

Senecaut, a senior budget analyst who also serves on Council 2's executive board, was chosen from 772 qualified people.

"I felt overwhelmed to be standing in front of my peers and to receive the award," she says. "What an honor to have been chosen."

Among the reasons she was cho-sen—Cliff Craig, the City's assistant finance director, said at an official award presentation April 19—is that Senecaut demonstrates the City's six corporate values.

• She is a person of integrity who will do the right thing even if it hurts;
• She cares about people, the departments and the City;
• She communicates, keeping everyone in touch;
• She is a team player, working with all departments, help-ing them to get their budgets together; she innovates; and
• She achieves. The City was particularly impressed with the way in which Senecaut conducts negotiations between labor and management.

"She has been seen as a voice of reason," Craig said. "That's an important role."

Such a role is challenging. Nego-tiations are often adversarial.

Yet Senecaut, with her dedication to honesty and fairness, has shown it is indeed possible to do so.

So much so that management has requested that she continue as president because they work so well together.

Employees with whom she works say she is courteous and kind.

Senecaut's dedication to reaching out to others does not stop at work. She also conducts volunteer work for the City of Seattle's Victims Support Team for victims of domestic violence.

2005

Emergency operator honored for heroism

A 911 operator, Cody Roberts, has been praised as a hero who saved the life of an East Olympia man earlier this year.

Roberts, who is Thurston County Communications Chapter Chair of **Local 618**, did so when he answered a 911 call from Sheri Ryan, whose husband Craig Thompson had collapsed unconscious on the floor.

Roberts walked her through the crucial steps — timed breaths and chest compressions — to keep Thompson artificially breathing. As she followed the steps, Ryan recalled her CPR training.

After a while, Ryan could feel Thompson's breath on her cheek as she administered artificial respiration. Roberts encouraged her to keep going.

Rescue workers arrived in minutes and took over.

"Thompson is alive today — and fully functioning — likely because of Roberts' persistence, patience and care in conjunction with Thompson's wife's actions," according to a report in *The Olympian* newspaper.

Roberts, 25, who was honored at a Real Heroes Breakfast in Lacey, was praised not only for his role in saving Thompson's life, but also for his assistance in another life-saving action.

He walked Nancy LaGasa through the steps of CPR so her husband, Bruce, could help a friend who also had suffered cardiac arrest.

Cody Roberts

"Cody was great," LaGasa said. "He was just very calm and thorough."

2007

Uniting LABOR and SCOUTING

Paul Hillestad

Paul (P.J.) Hillestad — maintenance technician for Pend Oreille County Public Works and secretary-treasurer of **Local 1135-P** — has been recognized nationally for bringing the labor and scouting movements together in his community.

He received the George Meany Award, approved by the AFL-CIO Executive Council, for his activities in the Boy Scouts of America and labor as well as for being active in his community in Newport, north of Spokane, to make it better for children.

Since he joined the Boy Scouts in first grade, Hillestad has been active in the movement, becoming a merit-badge, pow-wow and train-the-trainer instructor and providing outdoor leadership training.

Hillestad also is involved in his community in other ways. He is youth director at the American Lutheran Church in Newport, is a voluntary fire officer and secretary of the Newport Fire Department, an active member of Newport Kiwanis Club, and assistant head coach for the Washington State Special Olympics skiing team.

He earned a doctorate last year from the College of Commissioner Science.

How does Hillestad manage all these activities and yet find time to balance his community and family lives?

"The most productive people are the most active," says Hillestad "And it doesn't hurt to multi-task."

Hillestad maintains his calendar six months to a year ahead to ensure he meets all his commitments.

2007

Local president receives prestigious labor award

Susan Veltfort

Council 2's Susan Veltfort, president of **Local 1857** (King County Library System employees), has received one of the most prestigious awards in the Washington state labor movement.

Called the "Mother Jones Award," the award is given to a union member recognized as playing a major role in advancing the struggle for dignity and respect for working men and women in Washington State.

The award is named after Mary Harris "Mother" Jones, a legendary organizer for the United Mineworkers of America.

Washington State Labor Council, AFL-CIO, selects the recipient from 350,000 union members in the state. Veltfort is the first Council 2 member to win the award, presented over the last 13 years.

She was recognized for her courage and dedication to library workers within the King County library system and statewide over the last four years.

Veltfort was a prime mover in organizing Washington State's largest public library system — the King County Library System — in 2003, said Cameron Johnson, a library worker and Local 113 member, who nominated her for the award.

"Several past organizing drives had failed," Johnson said in his nomination.

"She was on the negotiations committee when Local 1857 negotiated its first-ever labor agreement in 2004."

Veltfort is also a founding member of IGLU, the Interest Group for Libraries and Unions, within the Washington Library Association, the state's premier organization for library workers.

2008

Named National Jail Supervisor of the Year

The prisoner was brought in to the Thurston County Jail on Christmas Day 15 years ago. Only 18, she was heavily under the influence of drugs.

One of the first people to see her was Deputy Sgt. Patty Smith, a medical liaison supervisor at the jail and member of **Local 618-CD.**

"I found out she had started drinking and doing heroin when she was 14," Smith recalls She had turned to stealing to get the money to support her habit. She had no diploma, nothing to show for herself."

Smith monitored her progress as the woman was sent to rehabilitation. "I got to know her grandmother and her mom and dad," Smith says. "It took two or three months to get her clean and sober. She later earned her GED and today she is happy, employed and doing well."

Smith can recall many such stories over the 37 years she has worked at the jail, 23 of them as medical liaison

Sgt. Patty Smith

officer. They are stories of inmates who kicked addictions while in custody and of lives that have been changed.

No wonder the American Jail Association honored her as Jail Supervisor of the Year.

It was only one of five national awards presented at a ceremony in Sacramento.

"I did not expect to receive an award of this magnitude," she said. "I like to work in corrections and to make a difference in people's lives. If they have medical problems or special needs, that's the part I like to do."

Smith says inmates are incarcerated for a variety of reasons and they are not all bad people.

"Some of them make mistakes, as we all do. We are all human and it takes a bigger person to try to turn them around."

"Don't give up on people," Smith says. "There is good in everybody. Look for it and you will find it. That will be a reward in itself."

2008

WHEN THE STORM HIT, WE WERE THERE

When a devastating storm brought widespread power outages, damage and flooding to the Pacific Northwest in early December 2008, Council 2 members sprang into action to help.

In many cases their jobs in road departments, waste water agencies, city government and sheriff's departments put them on the front line in providing relief.

Many worked around the clock to remove downed trees, restore power, maintain sewer systems and clear water-logged streets.

Others set aside their normal duties to assist victims, some of whom had lost everything in the floods. They linked them with aid agencies, handed out bottled water and helped in every way they could.

It was a time for emergency action. And Council 2 members showed they were more than up to the task.

Their rapid response and tireless work helped avert what could have been a far worse disaster.

Members of Pacific County Assessors Office pose with car damaged in storm. Front: Becky Nissell and Lisa Olsen, Local 367C secretary. Second row: Sheryl Crose, Loni Hooper, Local 367C executive board, and Connie Williams, Local 367C Labor Management Committee member. Third row: Dan Childress, Dennis Bryant, Local 367C shop steward and Bruce Walker, assessor.

2009

Outstanding job on snow removal earns workers unusual reward

Here's one for the record books: In late January, managers in Snohomish County served a free breakfast to 160 road maintenance employees and support staff.

They were saying "thank you" to the workers, most of them members of Council 2, for the outstanding job they performed in handling the impact of a series of snow storms followed by flooding that struck the county — and the rest of the Puget Sound area — in late December and early January.

"As far as I know, something like this breakfast has never happened before," says Roger Moller, president of **Local 109**, of which most of the employees at the breakfast are members. "I have worked here for 18 years and I have never had breakfast served to me by managers before.

"It was a fabulous breakfast. The managers prepared all the food and served all of it. All we did was go through the line and eat."

The managers were willing to reward the employees in this way because the road maintenance crews, fleet management and support staff had worked 16 days of 12-on and 12-off shifts, including working on Christmas Day.

They sanded roads, cleared snow and ice, cut and moved downed trees and ensured people could move around on all the major arterials as well as many side roads.

Moller points out, too, that they ran their equipment for 24 hours a day yet had no failures.

The performance was evidence of the great work that the mechanics perform in maintaining the equipment, he says.

The Local members received an additional recognition for the hard work they had performed under difficult circumstances, this one financial. They received 12 hours of holiday pay.

Hersey Award winners

The Hersey Award for exceptional service to the labor community has been presented at each biennial convention since 1997. It is named after Mary Hersey who was fired from her job at the Yakima Herald Republic newspaper for union activism. She successfully sued her employer and was reinstated, but quit the same day.

Hired by Council 2 as a staff member in 1972, she became the Women's Committee Advisor in 1980. She retired in 1992 and was presented with the first "Mary Hersey Award" shortly before she died in 1997.

Among the criteria taken into account in presenting the Hersey Award are:

• Advancement in leadership roles and/or activism within the labor movement.

• Outstanding service within the labor community.

• Service in a leadership role beneficial to labor.

• Service in a leadership role in coping with critical issues such as worker safety, minimum wage, comparable worth, human services, and political action needs.

• Participation in educational projects either through a local union or through another labor organization.

2001

Trina Young

'Typifies Hersey's qualities'

The Mary Hersey Award for outstanding achievement in Labor was presented by Council 2's Women's Action Committee this year to Staff Representative Trina Young, who represents Council 2 in Southwest Washington.

Young first joined Council 2 25 years ago as a member of **Local 275**, Grays Harbor County.

She was a state executive board member for 11 years and was hired as a staff representative in May last year.

She works out of the Lacey office.

Denny O'Neil, president of Local 307-VC, nominated Young for the award.

O'Neil, who works for the City of Vancouver, said Young typifies the qualities of Mary Hersey, after whom the award is named.

2003

Nancy Baker

'Always available'

Nancy Baker, member at large of the executive board of **Local 87** in Yakima, has received the Mary Hersey Award for outstanding service to the union.

Baker was cited for exemplifying the importance of being a union member, in particular for always being available for the tasks that needed to be undertaken.

In response, Baker said Mary Hersey, after whom the award is named, said if you want the union to work, you have to work.

"It is only as strong as the effort you put into it," she added.

2005

Vern Brown   'Most selfless person'

Many people in Yakima, particularly those who work for the City, knew him as "Mr. Union." Vern Brown earned the name for his active involvement in union activities over nearly 30 years, for his ability to recruit workers to the union, and for his organization of the annual Central Labor Picnic.

Brown, employed by the City of Yakima's Parks Department since 1974, is the first male to receive the Hersey Award. "Vern's passion for the welfare of his fellow employees throughout the City of Yakima has been second to none," Yvette Lewis, president of **Local 1122**, of which Brown was a member, said. "The interests of others came before his own. Where there was a cause Vern was there. He is the most selfless individual I have ever met."

2007

Terri Prather   'There when help is needed.'

When help needs to be given to a cause, Terri Prather is there to lend a hand.

"She is always willing to go the extra mile and always has time to help members," said Kathy Abernathy-Robinson of **Local 618**, who presented Prather, an operator at Thurston County's LOTT Alliance and Local 618 secretary, with the 2007 Mary Hersey Award.

Prather served in many union capacities, including treasurer of the Thurston-Lewis-Mason counties' Central Labor Council for seven years. Prather was fundamental in Local 618's "Helping Hands" project at Christmas, buying, wrapping and delivering gifts and meals to union families in need at Thanksgiving and Christmas time.

She also helped to organize the Local 618 summer picnic.

2009

Cherie L'Heureux

'Paid ultimate price.'

W hen employees at the Northshore Utility District believed they were being unfairly treated by management, fellow worker and warehouse inventory controller Cherie L'Heureux was among the first to step up and act on their behalf.

Over months, she — working with union members, including Council 2's Deputy Director Pat Thompson — took up the causes with management.

But — L'Heureux was to learn the hard way — management had not forgotten the role she had played in fighting for the rights of her co-workers. "When I was elected secretary of **Local 1024** in 2006 and took part in negotiations, that's when the pressure started to come down on me," L'Heureux recalls. "It became apparent that all my actions were being watched. On June 13, 2008 — yes it was Friday, the 13th — they fired me, saying they had found 13 errors and/or unauthorized changes to time sheets out of about 13,000 data entries."

"She paid the ultimate price," Thompson said when L'Heureux received the Hersey Award. "She is an inspiration to all of us in the union."

2011

Denny Finegan

'Calm, easy-going approach.'

D enny Finegan likes to support the underdog.

"I like defending people who have been done wrong, who have not been treated well," says Finegan, who works as a crew chief for the Thurston County Public Works Department and has been active in 700-member-strong **Local 618** for 30 years. He has served on Council 2's executive board for eight years.

"I like to make sure people are treated

decently. I enjoy it. It is rewarding."

"He is always there, helping people with their challenges in the workplace," Staff Representative Kathy Brown said when Finnegan received the Hersey Award. "His calm, easy-going approach to problem-solving is what sets him apart."

Finegan said receiving the award is humbling. "I will cherish it all my life."

Finegan works for the Thurston County Public Works Department where he began in 1981 after eight years working in the maintenance department of the Tumwater School District.

He has served as a shop steward, a chapter chair, and on and off as local president for 20 years.

What advice does Finegan give to someone entering public service?

"Stay active in the union," he replies. "Be aware there are people who want to get rid of unions and take away your job. We must retain our right to bargain collectively."

Finegan was appointed a Council 2 Staff Representative in 2013.

2013

Carol Travis　　'We work for we, not me.'

Carol Travis was unable to attend the convention in Spokane in June, 2013 at which she was presented with the Mary Hersey Award. So she left a note to be read at the ceremony. It said, simply: "We don't work for me, but work for we when dealing with management."

That note pretty well sums up Travis's approach to the union to which she has devoted so many hours. She served several terms as vice-president and president of **Local 874-H**, the local's executive board and the state executive board.

"I wanted to make sure everybody was able to be treated fairly," she says. "I was never out for myself. It was for the good of the people."

Her drive to be fair was tested when the Great Recession forced management to seek concessions from the union. "We would vote to defer pay raises for ourselves in order to prevent some of our members being laid off," she explains. "I would rather see other people being able to keep their jobs or even to keep the hospital open than insist that I should get my full pay."

Helping others

Our members give of their best for others

O ver the years, Council 2 members have reached out in a variety of ways into their communities around the state.

Whether it be raising funds to help others, replenishing a food bank, building houses or handing out Christmas gifts, they show they care. We are proud of these members of our union for the outstanding citizens they are.

Here is a selection of a few of the ways in which our members have reached out to others. Many such stories can be told and we know there will be many to tell in the future.

2002

Local members buy chess sets for detainees

Soon after Coreen Harty started working as a volunteer mentor for the Spokane County Juvenile Detention Center in October last year, she learned that the inmates enjoyed playing chess and had a competition each evening.

"But they had only two chess sets and so most of them could not play."

That set Harty — who is **Local 1553** Treasurer and a Genetic Testing Coordinator with the Spokane County Prosecutors Office — thinking of ways that she could help.

Officers of Local 155 pose with thank-you card from detainees. Standing, from left: Terrie Roberts, secretary; Amie Swenson, president; Deanna Walter, sergeant at arms; Michealanne O'Neill, vice-president; Coreen Harty, treasurer. Sitting: Wanda Clark, chief shop steward.

After all, it was not for nothing that she had been named "The Nicest Person in the State" for 2002 by the Washington Association of Prosecuting Attorneys.

Harty spoke with Darryl Robinson, a juvenile detention officer and member of **Local 492J,** who had taught the inmates how to play chess.

He said they would need 10 to 12 sets. "The sets that were needed were not inexpensive chess sets

you can pick up at most stores, but special competition sets that have clocks to time the plays and so on," Harty says.

Harty approached the Local 1553 executive board who raised $500 as a Christmas project and bought 11 sets.

The inmates were so grateful they drew a large "thank you" card, which they presented to the local.

2002

Pleasant surprise awaited member

When John Eaton was flown from Columbia County to Spokane for open-heart surgery in 2001, his fellow employees at the Columbia County Road Department (**Local 1191-CC**) knew that it would be a while before he would be able to chop and split wood again.

So, while Eaton was away, they cut up and split five cord of wood and hauled it to Eaton's home.

Members of Local 1191-CC split firewood to help a colleague who underwent surgery.

When Eaton arrived back, he was surprised — and delighted — to find his firewood was stacked and ready for his use during the approaching winter.

In wake of 9-11...
Show of solidarity with NYC workers

The AFSCME Women's Convention was scheduled to be held in Boston in November last year. But, in the wake of September 11, AFSCME president Gerald McEntee asked the organizers for permission to move the meeting to New York City as a show of solidarity with the City's workers.

Among those who attended were a dozen members of Council 2.

"The theme of the conference was a tribute to those AFSCME workers involved in the September 11 tragedy and subsequent rescue effort," says Alpha O'Laughlin, who attended the convention. One especially moving moment discussed the life and subsequent loss of Father Mychal Judge, an AFSCME member who died while administering last rites to a critically injured person.

"It was a really moving experience for all of us," recalls O'Laughlin.

2003

Olympia members go shopping for others

When members of **Local 618** developed their "Helping Hands" project for the holidays last year, they agreed that helping fellow union members would be appropriate.

"We discovered that there were two families right in our own local who were in need," explains Terri Prather, secretary of Local 618 and sub-chapter secretary, who works for the City of Olympia.

Local 618 allotted $500 and the Thurston-Lewis Labor Council donated an additional $250.

Prather and Paula Williamson, Local 618, City of Olympia chapter chair, bought items they felt would be useful and added a few fun items, too. Other union members donated food, clothing and gifts.

Christmas turned into a time of joy and surprise for families who had wondered where they would find money to buy their children gifts.

Santa (Mike Gallagher) with 7-year-old recipient.

Local helps organize fund raiser

After the September 11 tragedy hit, **Local 113** sought a way to help. They joined with the Everett Elks Lodge and sponsored a dance on November 24. Proceeds from the raffling of donated prizes went to the American Red Cross. Food barrels were filled for men's and women's shelters.

2006

Local president uses vacation to help Katrina victims

Pete and Loretta Seybert

When Pete and Loretta Seybert watched the drama of hurricane Katrina unfold on their television sets last year, they wondered what they could do to help.

They called the American Red Cross, explaining that Pete — president of **Local 1845-I**, Island County, and a volunteer firefighter with District 5 on Whidbey Island — and his wife, Loretta, are volunteer emergency medical technicians. The organization suggested they undergo additional training and put them on a fast track to give assistance to the hurricane-ravaged area of New Orleans.

By December they were ready to go. Pete decided to devote his vacation to the project and Loretta, an occupational therapist who works with children with disabilities up to age 3, set aside her scheduled time off to join him.

They left on December 13 and for the next three weeks each drove an emergency recovery vehicle (ERV) through the streets of New Orleans from Kenner, a suburb where the ERV staging area, the kitchen and supplies were located.

They delivered blankets, dry snacks and 500 to 600 hot meals throughout the day to needy residents in New Orleans neighborhoods.

"We worked from 7 a.m. to 7 or 8 p.m., announcing our arrival in an area with loudspeakers," says Pete.

Loretta says she was surprised at how much need there was in the area a couple of months after the hurricane struck the city.

"Many of the residents still did not have running water and gas," she explains. "The utility companies were still working hard to get them up and running."

The Seyberts say the experience was really rewarding and they would go back in a heartbeat.

2008

REACHING OUT

Union members help build houses for the community

It was a Saturday members of **Local 176-SW** will remember for a long time to come.

Rather than working in the yard, shopping, taking in a ball game or simply hanging out, they spent the day framing and building walls for a house.

The house was a project for the Skagit chapter of Habitat for Humanity, a worldwide non-profit Christian organization that builds affordable housing with the help of volunteers from all faiths and backgrounds.

"This is showing a sense of pride in our community," says Rob Macready, pres-

Members of Local 176-SW join other volunteers in building a house for Habitat for Humanity. Council 2 member Steve Huizinga is third from the left.
Top: Carrie Crisp of Local 176-SW works on the project.

ident of Local 176-sw and wastewater collection specialist at the City of Sedro-Woolley.

2008

Local members help food bank

When members of the executive board of **Local 1581** (Whatcom County Library System) learned that an area food bank was facing a shortfall, they encouraged members to contribute.

"With food prices rising, more people need help and the food bank needs more contributions," says Lisa Gresham, Local vice president.

Members of Local 1581 pose with some of their food drive results. They are (from left): Front row: Joanne Simonarson (steward), Kevin Harris (secretary), Zynet Schmid (steward) and Lisa Gresham (vice president). Back row: Karl Thompson (steward), Sarah Koehler (steward), Dianne Smith (steward), Patty Macheras (president) and James Weaver (treasurer).

Raising funds for children's center

Thirteen varieties of soup were served at a fund-raiser for the Children's Village, organized by **Local 433**, Lake City Employers Association in Coeur d'Alene, Idaho.

The Children's Village is a safe haven for children who are abused, neglected, homeless or in severe family crisis.

The soup lunch was the third fund-raiser held by the local for the home. About 70 people donated $300 and 200 pounds of food.

Keith Clemans, president of Local 433 (left) and Robin Ricks, vice president.

2009

Union members and FISH coordinators who took part in parking lot sale. Paula Hiatt (center) holds a check for the amount raised.

Parking lot sale helps residents

On August 15, 2009, **Local 792-CH** held a yard/parking lot sale to benefit FISH, a Kittitas food bank. Union members raised $459 for FISH and donated a television set to be used to educate clients on nutrition.

Habitat for Humanity also benefited from brand-new home building items and a local church benefited from a large amount of good quality clothing to give to those in need.

"All in all, it was a great weekend," says Local 792-CH President Paula Hiatt.

"Kittitas County employees helping Kittitas county residents in need."

Coat drive is a success

Local **1849-F** members at the Town of Friday Harbor held a successful coat drive recently to ensure nobody went without a basic necessity such as a coat this winter.

The staff invited residents to drop off clean and gently used coats and jackets at the town hall administrative offices, from where the San Juan Island Family Resource Center distributed them as part of the One Warm Coat community service project, free of charge, to local children and adults.

The drive resulted in 243 coats being dropped off at the offices, most of which were distributed to more than 90 San Juan Island families. Surplus coats were distributed on Lopez Island.

Index

C

D

E

F

K

Kanigel, Dave   62
Keenan, Bill   30, 38, 50, 53, 59, 66, 67, 71
Kent, City of   64, 91
King County Library   59, 66
King County Library System   94
King County Medical Examiner's Office   83
King County Prosecutors   22
Kinville, Sam   2, 7, 12, 16, 17, 19, 35, 41, 65
Kitsap County   48
Kittitas County   112
Kittitas County Road Dept.   10
Koehler, Sarah   111
Kootenai Environmental Alliance   44
Kremser, Norma   80
Kruckeberg, Carol   87

L

LaGasa, Bruce   92
LaGasa, Nancy   92
Lake City Employers Association, Coeur d'Alene   111
Laube, Harry   63
layoffs   19, 30, 57, 68, 69, 71, 72
Legislative Weekend   50
L'Heureux, Cherie   103
library pages   66
Lillo, Carlos   55
Local Government Collective Bargaining Act   16
Locals
  21   80, 81
  21-R   39, 46
  87   1, 5, 101
  109   1, 41, 61, 62, 98
  109-E   62, 78
  113   1, 108
  114   5, 31, 34, 49, 63, 89
  114-1   77
  120   1, 70, 87
  120-SCH   86
  121   5
  129   5
  176   14
  176-SW   110

M